The Book of Chowder

But when that
smoking chowder came in,
the mystery was delightfully explained.
Oh, sweet friends! hearken to me.
It was made of small juicy clams,
scarcely bigger than hazel nuts, mixed with
pounded ship biscuit, and salted pork cut up
into little flakes; the whole enriched with butter,
and plentifully seasoned with pepper and salt.
Our appetites being sharpened by the frosty voyage,
and in particular, Queequeg seeing his favourite
fishy food before him, and the chowder being
surpassingly excellent, we despatched it
with great expedition: when leaning back a moment
and bethinking me of Mrs. Hussey's clam and cod
announcement, I thought I would try
a little experiment. Stepping to the kitchen door,
I uttered the word ''cod'' with great emphasis,
and resumed my seat. In a few moments
the savoury steam came forth again,
but with a different flavour,
and in good time a fine cod-chowder
was placed before us. . . .
Fishiest of all fishy places was the Try Pots,
which well deserved its name;
for the pots there were always boiling chowders.
Chowder for breakfast, and chowder for dinner,
and chowder for supper,
till you began to look for fishbones
coming through your clothes.

—Herman Melville, *Moby Dick*

The Book of Chowder

Richard J. Hooker

Illustrated by Anna Baker

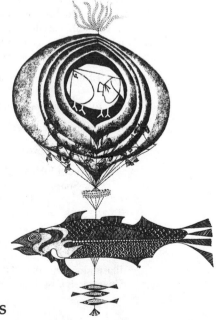

The Harvard Common Press

To Nancy

The Harvard Common Press
535 Albany Street
Boston, Massachusetts 02118

Printed in the United States of America

Library of Congress Cataloging in Publication Data

Main entry under title:

The Book of chowder.

    Includes bibliographical references.
    1. Soups.   2. Stews.   I. Hooker, Richard James,
1913–   I. Title: Chowder.
TX757.B58   641.8'13   78-18231
ISBN 0-916782-12-3
ISBN 0-916782-10-7 pbk.

Illustrations by Anna Baker
Cover design by Peter Good

Contents

Introduction

Chowder came to North America about two and a half centuries ago from a misty European background. In the New World it quickly won great favor as a delicious, hearty, easily made meal created from only a few ingredients. It became so well entrenched in the country's diet that it was carried across the continent by successive generations of American pioneers. In its movement through time and space it acquired ever new contents and characteristics.

But chowder had traveled even before it reached American shores. The beginnings of what would become American chowders may have appeared first in small French fishing villages, possibly in Brittany. From these chowder might have found a home on ships and in England. By the early eighteenth century it had reached Newfoundland, Nova Scotia, New England, and, in time, other English settlements to the south. These American landings could have been made in the company of immigrants from England or France or of sailors who had come to know chowder while sailing international shipping lanes.

So in any account of the early wanderings of chowder, facts must at times make way for supposition. That chowder was born in France was first argued in the nineteenth century. In 1869 *Notes and Queries*, an English periodical wherein correspondents pursued interesting topics, carried an exchange on the word *chowder*. One writer traced its origin to the French *chaudiere*, or cauldron. Another added that in ''the *cabarets* and *guinguettes* of little fishing villages along the coast of Brittany *ici on fait la chaudiere* is a frequent sign. *Faire la chaudiere* is to provide a cauldron in which is cooked a mess of fish and biscuit with some savoury condiments— a 'hodge-podge' contributed by the fishermen themselves, who each in return receives his share of the prepared dish.''

Fish, biscuits, and savory condiments would all appear in early American chowders, but just how *chaudiere* reached North America is not clear. Perhaps Breton fishermen, who had worked the waters off Newfoundland and Nova Scotia since the sixteenth century, carried the dish with them when they went ashore to dry and salt their catches before carrying them to European markets. Or, instead, chowder could first have moved from France into England and been taken from there to the American colonies. There had been close ties between England and France during the centuries that followed the Norman conquest. The French language flourished at the English court and among the aristocracy well into the seventeenth century, and French cooks were in demand even longer.

As early as the sixteenth century the words *chowder* and *chowter*, dialect variations of *jowder*, meaning a fish-seller, were known in Cornwall and Devonshire. By the mid–eighteenth century, and probably well before then, the English ate chowder. In 1762 Tobias Smollett had a character in one of his novels say, ''My head sings and simmers like a pot of chowder,'' and his final work, *Humphry Clinker*, contained a small dog named Chowder.

2

Still better evidence appeared in the 1763 edition of a leading English cookbook, Hannah Glasse's *The Art of Cookery*, which contained a recipe for ''Chouder, a Sea Dish'' (see page 28). In time the name would be loosely applied in England; a dish of corned salmon mixed with potatoes and baked was known about 1830 as chowder.

Hannah Glasse's designation of chowder as a ''sea dish,'' and a similar listing by Mary Randolph in her Virginia cookbook of 1824 (see page 33), suggest that rather than having entered North America directly from either France or England, chowder may have been known to seafaring men throughout the Atlantic world, coming ashore in many places to take on refinements and to flourish or wither as each new environment dictated.

The simplest chowders were certainly suited to shipboard fare, for until modern times sailors ate but few and coarse dishes. Ship galleys from the seventeenth well into the nineteenth centuries might store little more than hardtack, corned beef, salt pork, salt fish, and possibly some onions and other root vegetables. The cook could be of any nationality, for the crews were remarkably international with ''foreigners'' often outnumbering those of the country of the ship's registry.

Shipboard dishes were given various names—loblolly, lobscouse (an English name shortened in time to scouse), sea pie, burgoo, and chowder, among others. Such names were so loosely used that a given concoction might qualify under several. Most often served were stews, thick soups, and gruels, or, where a top crust was added, sea pies. The last—possibly intended for the ship's officers and favored passengers—closely resembled what came to be called chowders and consisted of salt pork and onions, fowl or veal, crackers or hardtack, and paste, all put down in layers with a top crust. Nantucket, it should be noticed in passing, would

3

have both fowl and veal chowders, and the former would flourish also on Martha's Vineyard (see page 55).

All sea dishes had to accommodate themselves to what was at hand. When the crew of the whaler *Pacific*, out of New Bedford, went ashore in a quiet cove in New Zealand in 1857 they took with them potatoes, biscuits, and a piece of salt pork. A fire was started, friendly Maoris collected mutton-fish, warreners, and limpets—all shellfish new to the crew—one man volunteered to act as cook, and all soon enjoyed an "excellent dinner" of chowder.

The first known reference to chowder in England's American colonies appeared in 1732 when a New Englander, one Benjamin Lynde, noted in his diary that he had "dined on a fine chowdered cod." Nineteen years later, in 1751, the *Boston Evening Post* published directions for making a fish chowder. The recipe, in verse, gave the basic elements for many later chowders—onions, pork, fish, salt, pepper, and biscuits. Herbs and claret provided additional flavoring (see page 27). Water was the cooking liquid, as would be the case for a century to come. Tomatoes were then almost unknown in the colonies, and potatoes were still very scarce. The use of milk or cream also lay far in the future. Publication of the recipe in a newspaper (a form of literature then restricted to relatively few readers), together with the use of wine and herbs, suggest that chowder had found middle-class sponsors.

In 1796 Amelia Simmons's *American Cookery* was published, the first cookbook to contain American recipes and ingredients. In a second edition of this work, published in 1800, there was a chowder of fish, pork, and crackers (see page 29). The only liquid was the water that the crackers had been soaked in. Covered closely, the dish was fried or stewed and was served with side dishes of potatoes, pickles, applesauce, or mangoes, and a parsley garnish. Strange as this very dry chowder might seem, it was acceptable to two other compilers of cookbooks who in 1805 and 1831 copied the recipe without comment or acknowledgment.

By the late 1820s there were new developments. A chowder in Lydia Maria Child's *The Frugal Housewife*, published in Boston, contained potatoes and, as an option, tomato catsup (see page 34). Potatoes would soon become common in chowders. Tomatoes, though known in parts of the colonies as early as 1770, were just becoming widely accepted in 1830, and tomato catsup was only then taking its first steps towards becoming the country's favorite sauce. The same decade saw clam chowder gain favor, together with the first, tentative uses of milk or cream in fish and clam chowders.

Although by this time chowder was known the length of the country, it was in New England that it flourished most. Here it was the object of the same careful and prideful preparation, with each detail important, as was then also given, in various parts of the country, to mint juleps, fruit pies, Marlborough pudding, gumbo, chicken salad, buckwheat cakes, and in the South to the curing of hams; or that would in more modern times be lavished on chili con carne, cheesecake, or the Martini cocktail. A Philadelphian in 1838 on his first visit to Boston related how he was invited to a home and ''duly initiated into the mysteries and merits of 'a chowder.' '' He tried both clam and fish chowders and could not decide which was superior. ''This favorite dish of the Yankees, I find, required no little skill in the making,'' he noted, ''and our worthy host informed me, that this was a part of the dinner which he never entrusted to his cook, but always superintended it himself.'' Individuals were famous for their chowders. Daniel Webster, who needed no additional glory, was among these, and in the 1840s told an early biographer how he made chowders (see page 38). His recipe, other than by combining the head and shoulders of a cod and a whole haddock, was not extraordinary. Still, when three men took a cruise along the New England coast in 1858 the captain of the chartered boat assured them that he could make a chowder as good as "Daniel Webster himself ever turned out."

The dish also received homage at chowder parties. These were seaside picnics at which chowder was awarded an honored place among various fish and shellfish. A clambake, with lobsters and corn accompanying the clams, might be included. Chowder parties were known in New Brunswick in the eighteenth century, for one was given there in 1786 in honor of H.R.H. Prince William Henry, the future William IV, then in command of a visiting naval ship. New England chowder parties may have come soon after, and by the early 1830s they were well established in the Boston area. A recipe of 1832 claimed to be "according to the most approved method, practiced by fishing parties in Boston Harbor." Those who chose could eat at numerous seaside fish, clam, and lobster halls, all of which served their "special" or "famous" chowders. Narragansett Bay was in time lined with such places. The South, too, had its chowder picnics and Joseph Baldwin, a writer on Southern customs, contended that "in the science of getting up and in getting through a picnic or chowder party, or fish fry, the Virginian, like Eclipse [a famed horse of the day], was first, and there was no second." Politicians used the festivity to gain or to encourage supporters, and in 1848 "a chowder" and clambake for ten thousand people was reported in Rhode Island.

Chowder may have reached the zenith of its popularity shortly before the Civil War. An English traveler in Massachusetts in the late 1850s admitted that though he did not care for the "odious compound" himself, it was "held in infinite esteem in these parts."

Well before this, regional and even local differences had begun to appear. The earliest chowders had used only fish, onions, pork, and crackers as the main components, with wine and herbs sometimes used for flavor. As tomatoes, potatoes, and milk crept into chowders, the opportunities for variety increased geometrically.

Nantucket Island, saturated with seafaring ways, had the simplest chowders, for here crackers, potatoes, milk, and tomatoes were all omitted. The fish, or clams, were joined with pork, onions, salt, and pepper, and thickened with flour and water (see page 53). When Herman Melville had Queequeg and Ishmael enjoy a clam chowder that contained pounded ship biscuits at the Try Pots Inn in Nantucket, he was either in error or reporting an aberration in that fishiest of all places.

Elsewhere in New England milk began to appear in chowders. A milky appearance was given even to water-based chowders by the use of flour and water or flour and cream to thicken the stew, and this may have led Harriet Martineau to believe that a chowder she ate in 1835 at Sandy Cove, Gloucester, was made with milk. Though water remained dominant, soon small amounts of milk or cream were added just before the dish was served, and by midcentury Mrs. E. H. Putnam, a cookbook editor in Massachusetts, noted that some cooks used half milk and half water.

Tomatoes, or tomato catsup, had been added to chowders, especially clam chowders, since the 1830s, though northern New England never embraced either. In parts of Massachusetts and in Rhode Island, Connecticut, New York, and other states farther south tomatoes were retained, sometimes with milk and sometimes with water.

Northern New England also increasingly left out the wine, cider, spices, herbs, curry powder, and other flavorings that had appeared in earlier recipes. Fish or shellfish, salt pork, onions, potatoes, biscuits, and water or milk became the standard ingredients, though either onions or potatoes might be completely omitted. A famous "genuine" chowder of Rye Beach, New Hampshire, was made without onions.

A minor regional difference appeared late in the century. In 1886 Sara T. Rorer of Philadelphia, a well-known editor of cookbooks, called for the dicing, rather than slicing, of chowder vegetables (see page 68). This practice gained some following everywhere, but was most common south of New England, especially for clam chowders.

Inevitably, so popular a dish as chowder attracted other principal ingredients. Eliza Leslie, an author of popular cookbooks, wrote in 1857 that lobsters, crabs, or oysters could be used in place of fish. Nantucket knew both chicken and veal chowders (pages 55 and 56). By 1879 catfish or hogfish chowders existed in Virginia (pages 58 and 60). About the same time, and probably much earlier, corn chowders were made as were others of potatoes, beans, parsnips, and other vegetables. Salt codfish had long served those who lacked access to fresh fish, and near the century's end a recipe was published for canned salmon chowder. Still more chowders were created in the early twentieth century, a time of lively culinary invention, some to win local success while others died at birth.

In the West, especially, chowders appeared that were quite unorthodox. In about 1900 Mrs. Lettie Lamkin in eastern Texas offered a chowder consisting of two Irish potatoes, three ears of corn, two tomatoes, one teacup of green peas, four pods of okra, and bacon "size of fist" all boiled together for an hour, after which two tablespoons of butter and salt and pepper were added. And in 1914 the cookbook of the Portia Club of North Yakima, Washington, contained a Spanish chowder: "Cut several raw potatoes in small pieces and boil with chopped or sliced onions; 1 can tomatoes; let cook slowly; when done add ¼ teaspoon soda,

1 quart hot milk and some grated cheese, salt and cayenne; serve immediately.''

To say when Manhattan Clam Chowder first existed would require a rigid definition. It may have descended from the chowders served during the late nineteenth century at Coney Island stands. In 1894 Charles Ranhofer, famed chef of Delmonico's restaurant, published a recipe for ''Chowder de Lucines'' made with pork, parsley, onions, potatoes (cut to seven-sixteenths of an inch square!), clams, tomatoes, and crackers, and flavored with thyme, salt, and pepper. A ''Fulton Market Style'' clam chowder of 1902 contained clams, onions, tomatoes, allspice, cloves, red pepper, and Worcestershire sauce (see page 80). A ''Vegetable Clam Chowder'' of 1929 had clams, chopped onion, diced carrots and potatoes, stewed tomatoes, and thyme. Very similar in content were two others in the same year, a ''Coney Island Clam Chowder'' and a ''New York Clam Chowder.'' All of these were certainly members of one family and all were radically different from the New England clam chowder. The word ''Manhattan'' may not have appeared on chowders until the 1930s or later; the first occurrence of this earthshaking event remains undocumented. Unwritten, too, is the history of the debate, usually conducted in terms of mock outrage, between the followers of the milk-based New England clam chowder and those who prefer the New York version made with tomatoes and water. Early Americans would, of course, have been astounded to be told that either milk or tomatoes could be used.

The twentieth century saw many changes in chowder making. Except among those who clung to orthodoxy, the use of salt pork declined or gave way to bacon or even corn oil, peanut oil, or butter. The liquid content of chowder grew, making it logical for cookbooks to list it as a soup rather than under the old heading of fish. Canned clams and fast-frozen fish eased the supply problem of many. On the other hand, overfishing everywhere and urban and industrial pollution of inland lakes and rivers and the oceans radically curtailed the supply of seafoods.

Chowders became more complex during the 1930s, a time of growing culinary sophistication, and again during and after the Second World War when innumerable American men and women were exposed to exotic forms of cookery throughout the world. Chowders appeared that contained not one fish or shellfish but a variety of seafoods, and there was a tendency to replace milk or water with a cream sauce or a carefully flavored stock. Various herbs and spices came into frequent use, some of them until then unfamiliar to most Americans: leeks, shallots, marjoram, oregano, paprika, and garlic, among others. This was a partial return to the earliest American chowders which had contained herbs, spices, and condiments.

Today, though degraded in many restaurants, the dish called chowder is alive and healthy. Numerous Americans in flight from the neat, easy, and uninteresting world of processed foods and fast-food restaurants have discovered that chowders, like other dishes made from the bounty of nature and the gardens of mankind, can contribute to the joy of living.

Suggestions on Chowder Making

Only an insensitive cook would repeat a recipe without attempting to improve it. When something like ''perfection'' is at last achieved, it is usually because science—in this case an accurately written and carefully tested recipe—has been abetted by artistry. The recipes that form the body of this book do not contain the final answer to all problems of chowder making, nor will any one of them satisfy equally all palates. They do offer an overview of the vast range and variety of chowders that have appeared in America. And they provide a point of departure for all who wish to move from familiar into uncharted country. All exploring, of course, should be done with an open and inquiring mind. Prejudice comports badly with research.

Except for the first three recipes and Daniel Webster's chowder of 1842, and for a few in which the directions are too uncertain to be followed with confidence, all the recipes in this book have been tested by the editor. Many other recipes have been tested and discarded as either of poor quality or repetitive of those retained.

Some editorial comment is inserted before each recipe. Here appear historical background and suggested modifications of the recipe. Where the quantities are too great for twentieth-century households, the amounts of each ingredient have been curtailed. The date given in the title of each recipe is the year of publication or, in a few cases, the year the cookbook was copyrighted. Most of the recipes antedate, by years or even decades, their appearance in a book. This is probably most true of the vegetable chowders, which may have led long, humble lives before being given the dignity of publication.

INGREDIENTS: FRESH OR OTHERWISE

As every intelligent cook knows, both flavor and nutrition are almost invariably best when fresh foods are used. Still, many people live far from the sea. It is comforting to realize, therefore, that excellent chowders can be made with frozen fish and shrimp, frozen or canned oysters, canned clams and lobsters, and so on. In similar fashion, some vegetables when out of season are available frozen or canned. Many an outstanding corn chowder has been made with canned corn.

FISH

Probably every edible fish, crustacean, or shellfish has at some time been used to make a good chowder. Early Americans preferred a firm, non-oily, white-fleshed fish—rating cod, haddock, or sea bass highest but giving friendly nods to blackfish, porgie, or tautog. Early in the nineteenth century a firm fish was preferred because large slabs or pieces of fish were put into the chowder kettle and were meant to be brought forth and served intact. Halibut, a delicious fish, was rarely used, but it can still make an excellent chowder, as can whiting, flounder, cusk, or hake, among others. Some Virginians made catfish chowders, and very good ones. The great Delmonico's restaurant in New York City, for nearly a century the country's model of excellence, made chowders of freshwater fish—eels, perch, or walleyed pike—and saltwater fish—sea bass, sheepshead, blackfish, or kingfish. Gulf coast residents have preferred red snapper, redfish, or sheepshead, though one Creole cook found pompano unsurpassed.

Inlanders discovered that many freshwater fish made good chowders, as well as the salt cod that for a century and a half was shipped everywhere by New Englanders as a low-cost staple. In 1864 the canning of salmon began on the West Coast, and soon chowders of canned salmon appeared. Then, in the 1930s, fish was fast-frozen, a boon to all who lived far from the sea.

No chowder maker should be discouraged by the lack of a particular fish specified by a recipe, for any other good chowder fish may be substituted.

BUYING AND PREPARING THE FISH

A fresh fish has an elastic flesh that if pressed will return to its original shape, reddish-pink gills, and eyes that are bright, clear, and bulging. And a really fresh fish has only a slight, and never an objectionable, odor. If the supermarket has enveloped fish fillets in plastic your duty is obvious: poke a finger through the plastic and smell. Any fish that you buy should have been packed in ice since it was caught and then kept in the coolest part of the refrigerator until used—and the sooner used the better.

Many early recipes state that the fish, usually one of four to six pounds, should be cut in slices or slabs, presumably bones included. Today, most people prefer to fillet the fish. In doing this, or having it done, the head, fins, tail, and bones should be set aside. These can be boiled for half an hour or more in a moderate quantity of water with a bay leaf, some peppercorns, a few sprigs of parsley, and a little salt to create a rich stock to be used in the chowder. The head of a cod—especially the cheek and ''tongue'' —contains much flavor, and New Englanders in the early nineteenth century served the head and shoulders of codfish as a party delicacy.

An alternative to filleting is to boil the entire fish, once it has been cleaned, for ten to thirty minutes, depending on size, until it flakes gently off the backbone, and the skin, fins, and bones can be easily removed. Again, the water in which the fish was boiled should be used in the chowder.

Salt cod must be thoroughly desalted before using. Cut the fillets into the size you wish and place the pieces in water. Keep these in the refrigerator while they soak, and change the water several times. After the salt, the preservative, is gone the fish should be used as soon as possible, preferably within a day. Any part of the desalted fish that is not used can be frozen.

An important injunction: when cooking salt cod keep the pot *below* a simmer. Anything more will toughen the fish.

CLAMS

Many kinds of clams are found along North American shores, but only a few reach the country's markets. Along the Atlantic coast from Greenland to North Carolina are the soft-shell clams, dug from sand or mud at low tide. Off the Maine and New Brunswick coasts and from Cape Cod to Texas are the hard-shell clams, given the Indian name of ''quahogs'' in New England and called simply clams, hard clams, little-neck, or round clams elsewhere. Florida's west coast has the Morton or trading clam. The Pacific coast knows best the razor, little-neck (unlike the Atlantic coast little-neck), butter, and pismo clams.

Soft clams should be tightly closed when bought. Discard any that have broken shells or that float. The best for chowder are those that lie out on the flats away from shore. Before use, the clams should be washed and scrubbed carefully to get rid of pieces of shell and sand. Clams can be opened with a clam knife while raw, saving the liquid to be added to the chowder. A much easier method to open clams is to heat them slowly in a closed pan with a few tablespoons of water until the shells open. Once the clams are removed from the shells, the long ''neck'' and the coarse membrane can be taken off. Quahogs can be opened by pouring boiling water over them and letting them stand for a few minutes before prying open the shells with a knife. Quahogs do not have a ''neck'' to remove.

Clams become tougher, rather than more tender, through cooking. Therefore, whatever any recipe might ask, do not add the clams to the chowder more than five minutes, or less if the clams are chopped, before the dish is to be served.

Should a recipe ask for more clam juice than your clams have provided, the difference can be made up by adding bottled clam juice or water.

CONCHS

These are available fresh in some southern Florida seafood stores, or canned in stores that deal in Italian foods. If bought fresh the conchs should first be trimmed of the black edge and tentacles. Then, because the meat is tough, it will have to be ground, pounded on a wooden board until it begins to fall apart, or tenderized in a pressure cooker for half an hour or more at 15 pounds pressure.

SHRIMP

It is important not to overcook shrimp. In the shells they should boil about ten to twelve minutes; if shelled, from three to five minutes.

PORK AND BACON, FATS AND OILS

For nearly three centuries Americans ate huge quantities of pork. The early settlers had discovered that hogs survived wilderness conditions well, multiplied rapidly, and were easily kept, and that their flesh salted successfully at a time of no refrigeration. Understandably, pork and lard found their way into almost every dish, from pastries to chowders.

Pork was put into chowders both because it was liked and to prevent the onions from burning in pots which hung over fires in the fireplace. In the 1837 edition of Eliza Leslie's *Directions for Cookery* she prescribed a pound or more of pork in her fish chowder. This was reduced to half a pound by her twenty-third edition eight years later. In the interim a good part of her readers had acquired stoves on which heat control was easier.

Today, many chowder makers remain devoted to small cubes of salt pork that have been fried to a golden hue. Others have found that bacon makes a satisfactory and easy substitute for salt pork. A suitable proportion might be two or three slices of bacon for each pound of fish. Once the bacon is crisp it can be removed from the frying pan and the remaining fat can be used to saute the chopped or sliced onions. The bacon itself can be crumbled and strewn over the bowls of chowder just before serving.

Chicken fat has an excellent flavor and was much used by Cape Codders. And there are some cooks who for reasons of health, convenience, or diet will omit animal fats altogether and use instead corn oil or some other vegetable oil.

ONIONS

Some recipes ask that onions be sauteed until golden or brown, but it is better to cook them only until they are limp and transparent. The proportion of onions to fish, clams, or other major ingredients is a matter of choice, but a medium-sized onion to each pound of fish could be used as a starting point. Slice onions on the bias to avoid rings.

SHIP'S BREAD, COMMON CRACKERS, ETC.

Some early chowders, like the similar sea pies, used one or more layers of dough. It is likely that at some point in the evolution of chowder, hardtack, or ship's bread, hard biscuits made of plain unsalted dough, were substituted for the dough layers. These replacements could have a rock-like texture and were, accordingly, soaked for a time in water to soften them.

A close relation of hardtack is the cracker variously named Boston, round, or common. Such crackers were used during the nineteenth century and are made today under the names of Cross and Bent, among others. They can be split and used to form layers within the chowder, or they can be broken into pieces for thickening. Soda crackers or oyster crackers go nicely with any chowder. Because they are salted, however, remember this when adding seasoning.

Croutons are good with many chowders, especially those with a milk or cream base. Simply cube some pieces of white, preferably stale, bread, and saute them slowly in butter or vegetable oil, turning them frequently, until they are crisp and brown. Croutons sauteed in bacon drippings make a fine addition to clam chowders. A crusty French loaf goes very well with any chowder and pieces of crisp, buttered toast are good with most. Bread sticks go nicely with all chowders. In Louisiana, corn pone is sometimes served with fish chowders. Finally, one can adopt a French custom and place a toast round in each flat soup plate, pouring the chowder over it.

THICKENING

Until recent times a chowder that had the consistency of soup was rare or unknown. Often the thicker parts of the chowder, when cooked, were removed to a platter or tureen, while the liquid remaining in the pot was thickened to a gravy by adding flour and butter, flour alone, or bread or cracker crumbs, before being poured onto what had been removed. In Thomas Cooper's recipe of 1824 bread crumbs were fried in the pork fat and then added in layers to the chowder as it was constructed in the pot. Sometimes thickening was provided by sprinkling a little flour over each layer placed in the pot, or by adding flour and water while the chowder was still cooking; and some chowder makers used mashed, rather than sliced, potatoes. Those who wish a soup-like, more liquid chowder can add milk, water, or stock at will. This, of course, also dilutes the flavor.

MILK

For about a century milk was nearly unknown in American chowders. Then it was added to some chowders in a small dollop just before serving, and not until the late nineteenth century did it become a large or the entire part of the liquid content, especially in New England. Today in conscienceless restaurants, of which there are many, milk alone is often used to expand a waning supply of chowder.

It is desirable to use whole milk in chowders, and it is sometimes well to substitute light cream for part of it. Once milk or cream has been added to a chowder, however, it should not be allowed to boil.

TOMATOES

Buy only tomatoes that have been ripened on the vine. Those picked green and gassed to a sickly pink have been foisted on the country by commercial growers and chain stores, and are quite unfit to eat in any form. A pinch or two of baking soda should be used to prevent curdling before milk and tomatoes are joined in a chowder.

If vine-ripened tomatoes are not available, canned tomatoes can be substituted.

STOCK

When a recipe calls for water as the principal liquid, added depth and interest can be given the chowder by using a stock instead. To a quart of water add half a cup of white wine, a small stalk of celery, a few sprigs of parsley, a piece of bay leaf, a small pinch of thyme, half a small onion, a half teaspoon of salt, five or six peppercorns, and the bones, fins, tail, and head of any fish. Simmer for about twenty minutes and strain. Should you lack any of the ingredients, use those that you do have. If it is the fish bones, head, and so on that are lacking, substitute a cup of white wine and a cup of clam juice for equal amounts of water.

Stock can be made in large quantities and frozen.

MUSHROOM CATSUP

Some older recipes call for this. To make a small amount take two pounds of mushrooms, chop them coarsely, and place them in layers in a bowl with a sprinkling of salt between each layer. Let stand for twelve hours and then squeeze them very dry in a cloth, saving all the liquid. Add to the liquid a few cloves and a pinch each of mace and allspice; let it boil until reduced by half; and then cool and bottle the catsup.

SALT AND PEPPER

In flavoring a chowder do not forget that salt pork, fresh clams, and crackers all contain salt. Pepper is important to a well-made chowder and should be ground fresh from a mill. White pepper goes well with any chowder and is especially needed, for the sake of apearance, with all milk-based chowders.

HERBS, SPICES, AND OTHER FLAVORINGS

Many people have been raised to believe that the only proper flavors of chowder are those of fish or shellfish, pork, onions, potatoes, milk, crackers, salt, and pepper. But through the centuries there have been experiments with other flavors, many of them highly successful. Early American recipes often called for mace, marjoram, cloves, curry powder, and other herbs and spices, sometimes with too heavy a hand. Garlic was generally scorned by the English and their American descendants, and only since the 1940s has it won some popularity in the United States among the general population. It is a fine addition to some chowders. Still other flavors can make a chowder interesting and different. Lemon, sliced thin, goes well with many chowders, as do on occasion thyme, rosemary, chives, parsley, cayenne pepper, pimiento, paprika, and Worcestershire sauce.

CREAM SAUCE

To make a cup of thin cream sauce, which is called for in some chowders, blend a tablespoon of butter with a tablespoon of flour in a saucepan over a moderate fire with slightly less than a half teaspoon of salt and some white pepper added. Separately scald a cup of milk, thin cream, or heavy cream with several slices of onion, a clove, a small bay leaf, and a few sprigs of parsley. After straining this milk, slowly add it to the butter-flour blend, stirring constantly. When the mixture has thickened, let it simmer a few minutes more. A richer sauce can be made by stirring a beaten egg yolk into it after it has been removed from the heat. Medium or thick cream sauces can be made by doubling or tripling, respectively, the amounts of butter and flour in the same recipe.

A simple cream sauce can be made by combining only the butter, flour, milk, salt, and pepper as indicated above.

WINE

Some early recipes call for claret or another red wine. Since few things are less appetizing than fish, biscuits, or potatoes stained red, it is better to use a white wine instead if a recipe asks for more than a small amount. A dry vermouth usually serves very well.

If a little sweet wine, such as port, sherry, or madeira, is required, add it just before serving.

LAYERS

Eighteenth- and early nineteenth-century recipes were designed for families, in which servants were sometimes included, of considerable size. A chowder could be expanded indefinitely by simply adding layers. Recipes today for four, six, or eight persons can ignore such layering with impunity.

SUBSTITUTIONS

Any good chowder fish can substitute for any other. In the same fashion, conchs and clams can replace each other.

Useful Measurements and Equivalents

In nineteenth- and early twentieth-century recipes, antedating measuring spoons, a spoonful usually means that any dry material should round as much above the spoon as the spoon rounds underneath.

A wineglass	=	¼ cup
A gill	=	½ cup
A dessertspoon	=	2 teaspoons
A saltspoon	=	¼ teaspoon
A pinch	=	slightly less than 1/8 teaspoon

CLAMS

36 soft-shell clams unshucked	=	2 pounds or 1 quart shucked
36 quahogs	=	two 7- or 8-ounce cans of minced clams
One 6½-ounce can of minced clams	=	½ cup of juice and slightly less of clams

24

LOBSTERS

4 to 6 one-pound live lobsters = 1 pound of meat

ONIONS

1 large onion, diced = 1 cup
1 medium onion sliced thin = ⅔ cup

POTATOES

1 medium-sized potato
sliced thin = 1 cup
1 medium-sized potato, diced = 1 ½ cups

TOMATOES

4 medium-sized tomatoes = 1 pound
3 medium-sized tomatoes = 2 cups

CARROTS

2 medium-sized carrots, diced = ¾ cup

CORN

1 ear, cut = slightly less than
½ cup kernels
7 to 8 ears, cut = 1 quart of kernels

CELERY

2 stalks, diced = 1 cup

CRACKERS

Boston crackers = common crackers = round crackers

A Boston Fish Chowder, 1751

This is the earliest known recipe for chowder in North America. The lack of any definite measurements would make its testing a matter of individual preferences. An error in the recipe is the use of onions to protect the pork rather than the opposite.

Experimentation could transform this into an excellent dish, though only an immense chowder would be able to use an entire bottle of claret or any other wine. Much better, for a smaller chowder, would be a small amount of white wine.

Directions for making a CHOUDER

First lay some Onions to keep the Pork from burning,
Because in Chouder there can be no turning;
Then lay some Pork in Slices very thin,
Thus you in Chouder always must begin.
Next lay some Fish cut crossways very nice
Then season well with Pepper, Salt and Spice;
Parsley, Sweet-Marjoram, Savory and Thyme,
Then Biscuit next which must be soak'd some Time.
Thus your Foundation laid, you will be able
To raise a Chouder, high as Tower of Babel;
For by repeating o're the Same again,
You may make Chouder for a thousand Men.
Last Bottle of Claret, with Water eno' to smother 'em,
You'l have a Mess which some call *Omnium gather 'em.*

From *The Boston Evening Post*, September 23, 1751.

An English Recipe for "Chouder, a Sea Dish," 1763

Hannah Glasse's The Art of Cookery, *where the following recipe appears, was first published in England in 1747 and went through many editions there. The work was republished in the United States in 1805 and 1812. The recipe given below comes from the eighth English edition of 1763.*

Here, as in the preceding recipe, is a framework on which an experienced cook might create an outstanding chowder, and certainly a unique one. ''Crimping'' refers to a practice known to the eighteenth century of cutting fishes in pieces while still alive, thereby causing the muscles to contract and making the flesh firm.

To make Chouder, a Sea Dish. Take a belly-piece of pickled pork, slice off the fatter parts, and lay them at the bottom of the kettle, strew over it onions, and such sweet herbs as you can procure. Take a middling large cod, bone and slice it as for crimping, pepper, salt, all-spice, and flour it a little, make a layer with part of the slices; upon that a slight layer of pork again, and on that a layer of biscuit, and so on, pursuing the like rule, until the kettle is filled to about four inches; cover it with a nice paste, pour in about a pint of water, lute down the cover of the kettle, and let the top be supplied with live wood embers. Keep it over a slow fire about four hours.

When you take it up, lay it in the dish, pour in a glass of hot Madeira wine, and a very little Indian pepper: if you have oysters,

From Hannah Glasse, *The Art of Cookery*, 8th ed. (London, 1763), p. 262. The recipe was reprinted, without credit, in P. Thornton, *The Southern Gardener and Receipt Book* (Newark, N.J.: A. L. Dennis, 1845), p. 138.

or truffles or morels, it is still better; thicken it with butter. Observe, before you put this sauce in, to skim the stew, and then lay on the crust, and send it to table reverse as in the kettle; cover it close with the paste, which should be brown.

Amelia Simmons's Fish Chowder, 1800

Little is known of Amelia Simmons, whose American Cookery *appeared in 1796 as the first cookbook of American authorship to be published in the United States. She claimed, however, to be an orphan who had little knowledge and but slight education. The following recipe appeared in the second, 1800 edition of her work. It could have been a "sea dish" known to New England fishermen, or it could have been copied from some English source. That it was fried, rather than stewed, makes it unique, though water from the soaked biscuits would have provided some moisture.*

Chouder

Take a bass weighing four pounds, boil half an hour; take six slices raw salt pork, fry them till the lard is nearly extracted, one dozen crackers soaked in cold water five minutes; put the bass into the lard, also the pieces of pork and crackers, cover close, and fry for 20 minutes; serve with potatoes, pickles, apple-sauce or mangoes; garnish with green parsley.

From Amelia Simmons, *American Cookery*, 2nd ed. (Albany: Charles R. and George Webster, [1800]), pp. 22–23.

Thomas Cooper's Codfish Chowder, 1824

Thomas Cooper, an educator, scientist, and agitator, was born in England in 1759, attended Oxford University, and in 1794 emigrated to the United States. Here, as a Pennsylvania supporter of Thomas Jefferson, he was appointed to the judiciary but left this to teach and to study chemistry at Carlisle, now Dickinson, College, and then at South Carolina College, now the University of South Carolina.

About ten good-sized portions of a very good chowder will result from this recipe. In testing, a slice of bread, crumbled, was used for each pound of fish, and the pork was diced. The vinegar-water-salt treatment of the cod was omitted. The wine-anchovy sauce alternative is not recommended, though Cooper's recipe for anchovy sauce is retained for anyone who wishes to attempt it.

Chowder.—Take fresh cod, and lay it in vinegar and water with a handful of salt in the liquer, all night. Cut it in pieces about the size of your hand, pepper and salt them moderately. For four pounds of cod, take one pound of thin slices of pickled pork; fry them till they curl, and are of a light brown colour; take them out, and lay them on a plate. Take about one-fourth of the fat that comes from them, and soak it up with crumbs of bread, and fry it of a light brown colour. Take an onion for every piece of cod fish; cut it into small pieces. Lay at the bottom of a stew-pan, a layer of the fried pork, sprinkle it with chopped onions and chopped parsley; on this lay a layer of cod-fish: on the cod-fish, a layer of fried pork, onions and

From Thomas Cooper, *A Treatise of Domestic Medicine . . . to Which is Added, a Practical System of Domestic Cookery* (Reading: George Getz, 1824), pp. 38, 66–67.

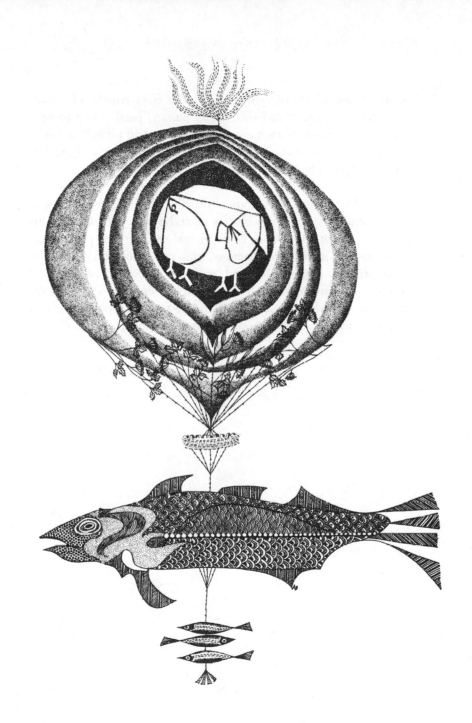

parsley; then a layer of split biscuit, with fried crumbs of bread. Then another layer of cod-fish, pork, onions, parsley and biscuit. Fill it up with water an inch above the surface; boil for half an hour. A tablespoonful of anchovy sauce, and one glass of wine, I think is a slight improvement, but not more.

Anchovy Sauce.—Anchovies usually come in green bottles in cases. Empty two of these bottles of anchovies, only leaving the chrystals [*sic*] of salt behind: to these, add too [*sic*] red peppers cut in pieces, the juice of two lemons, and six shalots chopped fine, some scraped horse-radish and a dessert-spoonful of flour of mustard. Boil altogether in half a gallon of Teneriffe wine, till the anchovies are dissolved. Strain and bottle for use. You may add or not, at pleasure, a pint of good mushroom-ketchup, and boil with it.

A Virginia Fish Chowder, 1824

It is possible that this recipe, taken from Mary Randolph's The Virginia Housewife, *was borrowed by her from some English cookbook. In any case, it makes a fine chowder. It was tested with two pounds of cod, a quarter pound of salt pork, diced, two medium-sized onions, ten soda crackers, and three-quarters of a cup each of dry vermouth and water. Most people will not wish to thicken it further.*

CHOWDER, A SEA DISH

Take any kind of firm fish, cut it in pieces six inches long, sprinkle salt and pepper over each piece, cover the bottom of a small Dutch oven with slices of salt pork about half boiled, lay in the fish, strewing a little chopped onion between, cover with crackers that have been soaked soft in milk, pour over it two gills of wine and two of water, put on the top of the oven and stew it gently about an hour; take it out carefully and lay it in a deep dish, thicken the gravy with a little flour and a spoonful of butter, add some chopped parsley, boil it a few minutes, and pour it over the fish; serve it up hot.

From Mary Randolph, *The Virginia Housewife* (Washington: Davis and Force, 1824), p. 99.

Lydia Maria Child's
Boston Fish Chowder, 1829

Lydia Child's The Frugal Housewife *went through thirty-two editions in eight years, appealing to housewives both for its recipes and its thrifty hints. But Lydia's main reputation was as an author, novelist, and abolitionist. She was so outspoken in behalf of the slaves that she aroused great hostility in New England and was even deprived of her free membership in the Boston Athenaeum.*

Her fish chowder is a fairly orthodox Boston chowder of the pre-milk era. It was tested with the following proportions to make six hearty servings, at least by twentieth-century standards: 2 pounds haddock; 5 slices bacon; 2 medium-sized onions; 2 medium-sized potatoes; 10 soda crackers, crumbled; 4 tablespoons of flour in 4 cups of water; 3 slices of lemon; and salt and fresh-ground pepper to taste. By the 1831 sixth edition of The Frugal Housewife *reference to a cup of beer was omitted.*

Four pounds of fish are enough to make a chowder, for four or five people;—half dozen slices of salt pork in the bottom of the pot;—hang it high, so that the pork may not burn,—take it out when done very brown;—put in a layer of fish, cut in length-wise slices, —then a layer formed of crackers, small or sliced onions, and potatoes sliced as thin as a four-pence, mixed with pieces of pork you have fried; then a layer of fish again, and so on. Six crackers are enough. Strew a little salt and pepper over each layer; over the whole pour a bowl full of flour and water, enough to come up even

From Lydia Maria Child, *The Frugal Housewife. Dedicated to Those Who Are Not Ashamed of Economy. By the Author of Hobomok* (Boston: Marsh & Capen and Carter & Hendee, 1829), p. 41.

with the surface of what you have in the pot. A sliced lemon adds to the flavour. A cup of Tomato catchup is very excellent. Some people put in a cup of beer. A few clams are a pleasant addition. It should be covered so as not to let a particle of steam escape, if possible. Do not open it, except when nearly done, to taste if it be well seasoned.

Eliza Leslie's Philadelphia Fish Chowder, 1837

Eliza Leslie was born in Philadelphia in 1787 and lived there until her death a few years before the Civil War. At some point in her early life she took a course in the cooking school of one Mrs. Goodfellow, got in the habit of giving friends recipes learned there, and eventually began to publish her own highly successful cookbooks. The following recipe, taken from the first edition of her Directions for Cookery, *was tested with two pounds of haddock, two medium onions, five ounces of salt pork, and eight soda crackers. The results were very satisfactory, as was another attempt that included a large potato, sliced. Eliza's recipe calls for a pound or more of salt pork, an amount reduced to half a pound by the 1845 edition.*

Take a pound or more of salt pork, and having half boiled it, cut it into slips, and with some of them cover the bottom of a pot. Then strew on some sliced onion. Have ready a large fresh cod, or an equal quantity of haddock, tutaug, or any other firm fish. Cut the fish into large pieces, and lay part of it on the pork and onions. Season it with pepper. Then cover it with a layer of biscuit, or crackers that have been previously soaked in milk or water. You may add also a layer of sliced potatoes.

Next proceed with a second layer of pork, onions, fish, &c., and continue as before till the pot is nearly full; finishing with soaked crackers. Pour in about a pint and a half of cold water. Cover it close, set it on hot coals, and let it simmer about an hour. Then skim it, and turn it out into a deep dish. Leave the gravy in

From Eliza Leslie, *Directions for Cookery; Being a System of the Art in Its Various Branches* (Philadelphia: E. L. Carey & A. Hart, 1837), pp. 55–56.

the pot till you have thickened it with a piece of butter rolled in flour, and some chopped parsley. Then give it one boil up, and pour it hot into the dish.

Chowder may be made of clams, first cutting off the hard part.

Daniel Webster's Fish Chowder, 1842

Writing from his home in Marshfield in October 1842, Daniel Webster outlined for an early biographer, S. P. Lyman, how he made a fish chowder. The recipe is quite lacking in details. Presumably the potatoes and onions were sliced, the salt pork diced, and the fish served in less than full size. As mentioned in the introduction, the head and shoulders of a cod contain much of that fish's flavor and made a popular party dish in New England in the early nineteenth century.

1. Fry a large bit of well-salted pork in the kettle over the fire. Fry it thoroughly.
2. Pour in a sufficient quantity of water, and then put in the head and shoulders of a codfish, and a fine, well-dressed haddock, both recently caught.
3. Put in three or four good Irish potatoes, for which none better can be found than at Marshfield, and then boil them well together. An old fisherman generally puts in two or three onions.
4. When they are about done, throw in a few of the largest Boston crackers, and then apply the pepper and salt to suit the fancy.

Such a dish, smoking hot, placed before you, after a long morning spent in the most exhilarating sport, will make you no longer envy the gods.

From General S. P. Lyman, *The Public and Private Life of Daniel Webster* (2 vols. in 1; Philadelphia: John E. Potter & Co., 1852), 2:63.

A Charleston, South Carolina Fish Chowder of Sarah Rutledge, 1847

Sarah Rutledge, daughter of Edward Rutledge, signer of the Declaration of Independence, published in 1847 a cookbook entitled The Carolina Housewife. *This contained her own recipes and others from "the family recipe books of friends and acquaintances," all presumably from Charleston and vicinity.*

The following recipe offers few specific quantities and only the vague direction to add "spices." It was attempted and found both fascinatingly different and delicious with the following: ¼ pound salt pork, cubed; a medium-sized onion chopped and sauteed in the fat until transparent; a pound of fish, and water to slightly more than cover it; 8 crumbled soda crackers; 3 shakes of cayenne pepper; a pinch each of mace and nutmeg; 4 whole cloves; a tablespoon of catsup; ¼ cup of Madeira wine; and salt and pepper to taste. Add the wine during the last half minute of cooking. Serves four.

Cut the fish into pieces, and wash them well. Fry some chopped onions with rashers of pork. Put the fish into a saucepan, with water sufficient to cover it. Thicken it with three or four sailor's buiscuits [*sic*], and season it to your taste, with cayenne pepper and spices. When nearly done, add ketchup and wine to flavor it; a pint or more, according to the quantity you make. It takes one hour from the time it is put into the saucepan; but if the quantity is large, it will require more time.

From Sarah Rutledge, *The Carolina Housewife, or House and Home: by a Lady of Charleston* (Charleston, S.C.: W. R. Babcock & Co., 1847), pp. 52–53.

A New England Fish Chowder with Milk and Tomatoes, 1851

By the mid–nineteenth century not only was milk increasingly entering American chowders but the country was also fast developing its love affair with the tomato. Both appear in this 1851 recipe and the combination was to find a lasting home in parts of southern New England, though water was frequently substituted for the milk. This particular chowder is delicious. It was tested to make two servings with ¼ pound of salt pork, diced small; a medium-sized onion; a pound of fish; 2 cups of milk; 2 medium-sized tomatoes, peeled and chopped; and 5 common crackers or 10 soda crackers. A pinch of baking soda was added before the milk and tomatoes were joined to prevent curdling. Most modern cooks will prefer to cut up the fish rather than to retain large slices.

Chowder. Try out some slices of pork, crisp, and then brown well some two or three onions. Cut your fish into three or four pieces, not slices. Pour over the onions and pork some milk or milk and water, with a little salt and pepper. Let this boil up, then put in the fish carefully, with some fresh tomatoes or tomato catchup. Cover it well, and let it simmer about one half hour. Have ready some crackers, split and swelled in cold water; lay them over the fish, and cover again for another fifteen or twenty minutes. Turn around your pot very often, that it might not burn. When cooked, remove the crackers, and with a slice and spoon take up each piece of fish unbroken, laying it on the dish, to be served in its natural form. Pour the liquid into the tureen, to be served hot. The crackers can be served on a separate dish, or put into a tureen. Some persons like the flavor of mace and cloves, and some claret wine.

From *The American Matron; or, Practical and Scientific Cookery* (Boston: James Munroe & Co., 1851), pp. 173–74.

Eliza Leslie's "Yankee Chowder," 1857

The Philadelphian Eliza Leslie must have gone to a good source for this "Yankee" chowder, for the result is outstanding. It was tried with the following quantities to make four medium-sized servings: ¼ pound salt pork; 2 medium-sized onions; 2 eight-ounce bottles of clam juice plus a small amount of water; a pound of fish; a medium-sized potato; and 10 soda crackers. About half the fat from the pork or bacon is adequate, and most people will prefer to slice, rather than to quarter, the potato.

YANKEE CHOWDER.—Having sliced very thin some salt fat pork, season it with pepper, lay it in the bottom of a large iron pot, set it over the fire, and let it fry. When done, take out the pork, leaving the liquid fat in the bottom. Next, peel and slice some onions, and lay them on the fat. Pour in sufficient clam or oyster liquor to stew the onions. Have ready a sufficient quantity of sea-bass, black fish, tutaug, porgie, haddock, or fresh cod. Cut the fish in small pieces, and put it into the pot. Add plenty of potatoes pared and quartered. Then some clam liquor; and lastly, some crackers, (soaked and split) or some soda biscuit; the crackers to cover the top. If you wish to fill a large pot, repeat all these ingredients, arranging them in layers. If there is not gravy enough, add some boiling milk, poured in at the last, and enriched with bits of butter mixed with flour. Cover the pot closely, and let it stew half an hour, or more, till all the contents are thoroughly done. You may bake the chowder in an iron oven, over a wood fire, heaping live coals on the oven lid.

From Eliza Leslie, *Miss Leslie's New Cookery Book* (Philadelphia: T. B. Peterson and Bros., 1857), pp. 88–89.

Commodore Stovens's Fish Chowder, 1857

Eliza Leslie does not identify Commodore Stovens, whose recipe she offers, but he was clearly able to make a good chowder. It can be made with any chowder fish and is excellent without the mushroom catsup if that is not at hand. Do not, however, substitute tomato or any other catsup in its place. As for the port wine, this is very much a matter of taste. It is best to omit it until the chowder is finished. Then try a small amount of chowder with a dash of port and decide from there whether to add some or omit entirely. The recipe makes about ten servings.

FINE CHOWDER.—This is Commodore Stovens's receipt:— Take four table-spoonfuls of minced onions that have been fried with slices of salt pork; two pilot-biscuits broken up; one table-spoonful of minced sweet marjoram, and one of sweet basil; a quarter of a bottle of mushroom catsup; half a bottle of port wine; half a nutmeg grated; a few cloves, and mace, and pepper-corns; six pounds of fresh cod, and sea-bass, cut in slices. Put the whole into a pot, with water enough to cover it about an inch. Boil it steadily for an hour, carefully stirring it. Serve it up hot in a large deep dish.

From Eliza Leslie, *Miss Leslie's New Cookery Book* (Philadelphia: T. B. Peterson and Bros., 1857), p. 88.

A Shaker Perch Chowder, ca. 1860

The Shakers did not have a distinctive cookery, but their fine herds of cows and their carefully tended gardens of herbs and vegetables provided the wherewithal for excellent meals. It was likely, too, that in their communities the best cooks gravitated to the kitchens. This rich and delicious chowder—using wine, spices, herbs, butter, cream, and a variety of vegetables—is evidence enough that the austerity of Shaker life did not extend to the dining table. The recipe comes from a manuscript in the Shaker Museum, Old Chatham, New York. It can be made with any fish.

4 ½ pounds perch
¼ cup good sherry or cider
1 teaspoon dried thyme
2 whole cloves
½ teaspoon salt
½ teaspoon pepper
½ cup thinly sliced onions

⅓ cup well-scraped cut-up celery stalk
½ cup carrot cubes
1 teaspoon chopped green pepper
3 teaspoons butter
2 cups heavy cream

From the meat of the fish, fillet at least 1 ½ pounds of boneless strips and cut into 2 inch lengths. Cover with sherry or cider and let stand 30 minutes. Cut remainder of fish in pieces, put in a kettle with water to cover, add thyme, cloves, salt, and pepper. Simmer 30 minutes and cook vegetables in the fish broth until tender. In the meantime gently simmer the strips of perch in 3 teaspoons of butter 5 to 10 minutes, but not longer as they must hold shape. Combine fillets with braised vegetables. Scald cream and add. Serves four.

A New Bedford Fish Chowder, 1859

In that this simple chowder is flavored by salt pork and onions but omits the solid parts of both, it anticipates the later chowders of Mary J. Lincoln and her student, Fannie Farmer. When ready to be served, this chowder contains only fat, fish, potatoes, water, salt, pepper, and a thickening of flour and cream. Like Nantucket chowders of the time it contains no biscuits or crackers; unlike them, it does contain potatoes.

The following makes six servings of this fine chowder: 3 slices of bacon; 2 medium-sized onions; 2 pounds of fish; 2 medium-sized potatoes, sliced; water to cover; and a tablespoon of flour in ¼ cup of cream, with salt and red or black pepper. As the title indicates, clams may be substituted for fish.

Chowder of Fish or Clams

Cut in slices some pork, try out the fat, put in two or three onions sliced, brown these and take all out but the liquor, skin the fish, cut it up, season all with salt, red or black pepper. Peal and slice some potatoes, add with boiling water enough to cause them to boil about one half an hour, or until the potatoes and fish are done; thicken it with about two table-spoons full of flour in a gill of cream.

From P. H. Mendall, *The New Bedford Practical Receipt Book* (New Bedford: Charles Taber & Co., 1859), pp. 20–21.

Mrs. Goodfellow's Philadelphia Fish Chowder, 1865

Mrs. Goodfellow was a famed teacher of cooking in Philadelphia; it was in her school that Eliza Leslie, several of whose recipes appear in this book, began her career. Although Mrs. Goodfellow was most active during the first half of the nineteenth century, her cookbook did not appear until 1865.

The chowder below is absolutely first-rate but it is very, very thick. In the test the clam liquor was increased. To make four servings: 3 slices of bacon; 2 medium-sized potatoes sliced very thin; a pound of fish; 2 medium-sized onions sliced thin; half a lemon sliced very thin; 12 rolled soda crackers; 2 pints of bottled clam juice; and a tablespoon of flour mixed with a cup of cold water. Do not forget the lemon, for it adds an important flavor.

Slice thin some fat salt pork, fry them brown and crisp; take out the slices of pork, then slice some white potatoes and lay them in the saucepan in which the pork was browned, then cut into slices some fish, (any kind of rich juicy fish will answer,) flour them and sprinkle with a little salt and pepper, then have ready some fried slices of onions and lay them on the fish, then grated crackers and a fresh lemon thinly sliced, then some of the pork, then fish, sliced potatoes, seasoning, a little more onion, and then the rest of the pork; on the top strew very thickly grated or powdered crackers, and over the whole pour a pint of clam or oyster juice—clam is the best. Then mix in a bowl, two tablespoonsful of flour and half a pint of cold water very smoothly, pour it over the whole. It must be covered up and not opened until cooked, which must be done slowly in three-quarters of an hour. Serve very hot.

From *Mrs. Goodfellow's Cookery As It Should Be* (Philadelphia: T. B. Peterson & Bros., 1865), pp. 128–29.

Elizabeth H. Putnam's "Club Chowder," 1869

A far cry, this, from the simple chowders of the early nineteenth century, but delicious. The recipe as given makes about 36 servings. To make four servings, use 2 cups of stock or water; 2 potatoes, mashed; 1 large onion, sliced; about 8 soda crackers; 2 slices of bacon; 1 ¼ pounds of fish; ½ tablespoon of parsley, chopped; 1 tablespoon of butter; a pinch each of ground cloves and ground nutmeg; a few sprigs of thyme or savory; a teaspoon of lemon juice; a lump of sugar; a quarter cup of sherry or Madeira; and salt and pepper to taste. Cook, covered, over a very low fire. The color will be more beige than dark brown. Follow the directions carefully and the result will delight you.

Have prepared the following: A good stock from veal or beef; water will answer, but the chowder is better with stock. Boil twelve potatoes, and mash them. Slice and fry brown six large onions. Soak two ship or other hard biscuit soft. Fry four slices of pork cut in small dice. Cut in slices about an inch thick eight pounds of fish: cod, sea-bass, haddock, or black fish are the best. Have chopped fine three table-spoonfuls of parsley.

Have a pot capable of holding three gallons, in which first put five or six table-spoonfuls of butter; scatter over one half of the fried onions; add a table-spoonful of salt, a teaspoonful of black pepper, a teaspoonful of grated nutmeg and ground clove mixed. Put in a layer of fish, and then a layer of mashed potato, and one half the biscuit; add a bouquet of thyme or summer savory; repeat

From Elizabeth H. Putnam, *Mrs. Putnam's Receipt Book* (New York: Sheldon & Co., 1869), pp. 230–31. Sixteen years later this recipe was copied, without credit, in Christian Woman's Exchange, *The Creole Cookery Book* (New Orleans: T. H. Thomason, 1885), pp. 229–30.

the same operation, leaving out the spice and thyme. Then pour in your stock or water, sufficient to cover the fish about four inches; add the parsley, also the juice of a lemon, squeezed into a tumbler of water in which you have dissolved four or five lumps of sugar. Place it on the fire, and let it cook gently an hour and a half. Color the chowder a dark brown. It should be of the consistency of calf's head soup. If too thin, thicken it with a little flour and water. The fried pork you can add before it is served, if you fancy it. I never use it. Just before serving, add a small tumbler of Madeira or sherry.

Preserved mushrooms, clams, or oysters add to the flavor. If the quantity of spice does not suit the taste, add as much more as you please.

A Fish Chowder
of the Parker House, Boston, 1873

Creole cooks of New Orleans frequently borrowed good recipes from various parts of the United States, and Celestine Eustis, preparing a cookbook at the beginning of the twentieth century, was no exception. Among her recipes was one for fish chowder as made, she noted, on September 23, 1873, at Boston's famed Parker House.

The recipe is unusual in two ways: it is remarkably "dry," and it uses raw, rather than fried, onions. When made with the liquid content called for, its consistency would be about that of corned-beef hash and it could be heaped up on a plate. In the following conversion to a recipe for two persons, the liquid content is increased: 1 pound cod, haddock, or similar fish; 1 medium-sized potato; 1 medium-sized onion; ¼ pound salt pork; 1½ cups water; and ¾ cup milk. Be sure that the flame is very low under the covered pot.

Have a fresh, firm cod or haddock, a fish about five pounds is the best size. Take saucepan large enough to hold a little more than you wish to make. Cut salt pork in small squares about the size of dice, and fry quite brown. Lay in the same pan alternate layers of thin sliced potatoes first, then slices of fish, then broken water crackers, small fried pork, shreds of raw onion, black pepper and salt to suit the taste. Continue the layers until you have used up your material. Pour over it the pork fat from the scraps and half a pint of water, to keep from burning at the bottom. Close the

From Celestine Eustis, *Cooking in Old Creole Days* (New York: Russell, 1903), pp. 22–23.

saucepan tight and set on the fire. Cook slowly, without stirring, for forty-five minutes, when it is ready for the table. As some fish cook drier than others, if you do not find the chowder thin enough to serve well in tureen, add some fresh milk just before taking up, and let it come to a boil.

A Nantucket Fish Chowder, 1874

Until modern times a stark simplicity characterized the meals on Nantucket Island. A visitor there in the late eighteenth century described the diet of a large family as consisting mainly of clams, oysters, and Indian corn bread, though there was a good supply of smoked bacon. Larger fish, when caught, were "a source of dainties."

A century later this fish chowder, and the following Nantucket chicken, veal, and potato chowders were certainly presented as "dainties." Today, however, they have little appeal and are presented in this book more for their historical interest than for use. All but the potato chowder, incidentally, omit both potatoes and biscuits—apparently a characteristic of the island's chowders.

This fish chowder recipe probably assumes about two pounds of fish to make four servings.

For a medium-sized codfish take about one-half pound of clear salt pork. Cut the pork into slices. Fry it till crisp. If you have a large *round-bottomed* pot to bake the chowder in, it is well to begin by frying the pork in it. But if you only have the ordinary range pots, a spider will be more convenient for frying. When the pork is crisp and brown, take it out of the fat, and put into the fat two or three onions sliced. Let the onions fry till brown, being very careful not to let them burn. Stir them well and they will not burn. A sure way to prevent burning is to add a little boiling water to the fat before the onions are put in. But then the onions will not brown, and you cook them till soft. If you have fried in a spider or frying-pan, turn

From *Nantucket Receipts. Ninety Receipts Collected Chiefly from Nantucket Sources* (Boston: Roberts Brothers, 1874), p. 335.

the onions, when done, into the pot in which the chowder is to be made; pour in the fat also, but do not put the pork in unless you like it. If you like the pork, it is best to chop it fine before frying. Cut your fish up into convenient pieces. Put them into the pot with the fat and onions. Pour in boiling water till the fish is covered and the water stands three or four inches above it. As the water boils away add a little, boiling hot. Boil till the fish is done,—about twenty minutes. Then pour in the thickening and let it boil up once or twice more. The thickening is made by mixing three heaping table-spoonfuls of flour very smoothly with a little water. Add the water very gradually, and rub the flour into a fine, smooth paste. When perfectly smooth and fine add one-half pint more of water, or milk if you like; season it plentifully with salt and pepper and turn it into the chowder, stirring it well in. Let it boil up once and the chowder is done.

A Nantucket Chicken Chowder, 1874

Anyone trying this chowder may find it desirable to remove the chicken, after it is cooked, and debone and dice it before returning it to the chowder. Martha's Vineyard, it should be noted, also had a chicken chowder.

Buy chickens or fowls. One good-sized fowl will make a pot of chowder. Cut it as for stewing. Put it into the pot, with water enough to cover it, and three or four inches over. Keep about the same amount of water by filling up with boiling water. But don't fill up too much. Boil gently till the chickens are tender.

Fry pork and onions as for fish chowder, but don't put them into the pot till the chickens are nearly done, and don't put in all the fat. If the chicken is very fat itself, the onions alone may be put in, as enough fat will cling to them. Finish the chowder with thickening, just as in fish chowder. But if considerable fat stands on top of the chowder, skim off some of it before the thickening is put in. It will take two or three hours to cook the chickens, according to their age and size.

From *Nantucket Receipts. Ninety Receipts Collected Chiefly from Nantucket Sources* (Boston: Roberts Brothers, 1874), p. 36.

Nantucket Potato and Veal Chowders, 1874

These recipes refer for detail to the preceding fish and chicken chowders of Nantucket. It is possible that the existence of a potato chowder on the island—a dish that would have been very simple, economical, and possibly all too common—explains why potatoes were omitted from other chowders. Both the potato and veal chowders could be greatly improved, of course, by substituting a flavored stock for the water, but they would then no longer be Nantucket chowders.

For potato chowder, use pork with a little lean on it. Chop the pork fine, or cut it into little dice. Fry with onions as above [see the Nantucket Chicken Chowder recipe], and put pork, fat, and all into the pot. Peel the potatoes, cut them into slices, say four slices to a medium-sized potato. Put in considerable water. Thicken and season as in fish chowder. Veal also makes a very good chowder. Cut lean veal into small pieces, and make it like chicken chowder. There should be water enough in all these chowders to have much more liquid than meat.

From *Nantucket Receipts. Ninety Receipts Collected Chiefly from Nantucket Sources* (Boston: Roberts Brothers, 1874), p. 36.

Mary Terhune's Clam Chowder, 1878

Mary Virginia Hawes Terhune, born in Virginia and married to the Reverend Edward Payson Terhune, published Common Sense in the Household *in 1871 and* The Dinner Year-Book *seven years later. These and other of her cookbooks appeared under the pseudonym of Marion Harland.*

This clam chowder was attempted and turned out well, for four, with the following quantities: ¼ pound of salt pork; 2 medium onions; 4 common crackers split and soaked in milk; 3 cups of water; 20 clams and their liquid; ¼ cup of dry vermouth; a teaspoon of catsup; 8 rolled soda crackers for thickening; and 4 thin slices of lemon. The clams, chopped, were not added to the pot until the last few minutes.

Fry five or six slices of fat salt pork crisp, and chop fine. Sprinkle a layer in the bottom of a pot; cover with clams; sprinkle with pepper, salt, and bits of butter, then with minced onion. Next, have a stratum of small crackers, split and soaked in warm milk. When the pot has been filled in this order, cover all with cold water, and cook slowly (after the water is heated) three-quarters of an hour. Strain the chowder, without pressing or shaking; put clams, etc., into a covered tureen; return the liquor to the pot. Thicken with rolled crackers; add a glass of wine, a tablespoonful of catsup; boil up, and pour over the chowder. Pass sliced lemon with it.

From Marion Harland, *The Dinner Year-Book* (New York: Charles Scribner's Sons, 1878), pp. 207–8.

A Virginia Catfish Chowder
of Mrs. Philip T. Withers, 1879

Mrs. Withers of Lynchburg contributed the following recipe for publication in Marion C. Tyree's Housekeeping in Old Virginia. *It was found excellent with the following: a pound of catfish meat; 2 tablespoons of butter; a cup of light cream; a medium-sized onion; a teaspoon of English mustard; a tablespoon of tomato catsup (for lack of walnut catsup), a few slices of lemon; salt and pepper; a pinch of baking soda; and a cup of stock from the cooking of the catfish. The cream was added at the very last. Makes two servings.*

To be made of New River cat-fish.

Wash the fish in warm water, put it on in just water enough to cover it, boil until tender or until the bones will slip out; take out the largest bones, chop up the fish, put it in a stewpan with a pint of water, a large lump of butter.

1 cup of cream, pepper and not much salt.

1 onion, one teaspoonful mustard, one-half teacupful walnut catsup.

Stew until quite thick, garnish with sliced lemon and serve hot.

From Marion Cabell Tyree, *Housekeeping in Old Virginia* (Louisville: John P. Morton and Co., 1879), p. 99.

A Virginia Catfish Chowder
of Miss Fannie Nelson, 1879

Fannie Nelson of Yorktown, Virginia also contributed a catfish ("or hog-fish") chowder to Marion Tyree's cookbook. Although quite different from the preceding recipe, it is at least as good. It was tried, for two servings, with the following: a pound of catfish meat; a medium-sized onion; 2 tablespoons of butter; salt and fresh-ground pepper; a tablespoon of Worcestershire sauce; a tablespoon of fine-chopped celery; 2 pinches of thyme; a few sprigs of parsley, chopped; and 2 cups of stock from the cooked catfish.

Take two cat-fish, skin, and boil till thoroughly done; pick very fine and add:

> 2 good sized onions
> ¼ pound butter
> 1 tablespoonful salt
> 1 tablespoon pepper
> 2 tablespoonfuls Worcestershire sauce.

Add a little celery or celery-seed, a little thyme, a little parsley.

Pour over all about one quart of boiling water and cook fast about half an hour.

From Marion Cabell Tyree, *Housekeeping in Old Virginia* (Louisville: John P. Morton and Co., 1879), p. 99.

Mary Terhune's Fish Chowder, 1880

*As a Virginian, Mary Terhune followed Southern customs in this
recipe by using water as the liquid and spices for flavoring, together
with oysters and oyster liquor. The spices and the catsup should be
used very lightly to prevent their overwhelming the fish and
oysters. This recipe makes twelve to fifteen very enjoyable
servings.*

Slice six large onions, and fry them in the gravy of fried salt pork.
Cut five pounds of bass or cod into strips three inches long and one
thick, and line the bottom of a pot with them. Scatter a few slices
of onion upon them, a little salt, half a dozen whole black peppers,
a clove or two, a pinch of thyme and one of parsley, a tablespoonful tomato or mushroom catsup, and six oysters; then comes a layer
of oyster crackers, well-soaked in milk and buttered thickly.
Another layer of fish, onions, seasoning, and crackers, and so on
until all are used up. Cover with water, boil slowly for an hour and
pour out. Serve with capers and sliced lemon. A cup of oyster liquor
added to the chowder while boiling improves it.

From Marion Harland, *Common Sense in the Household: a Manual of Practical
Housewifery*, rev. ed., (New York: Charles Scribner's Sons, 1889), pp.
56–57. This work was copyrighted in 1880.

Mary J. Lincoln's Boston Fish Chowder, 1884

Mary Johnson Bailey Lincoln was the first head of the famous Boston Cooking School. There, from 1879 to 1885, she not only laid down guiding principles for this and other similar schools but had also a large influence on at least one of her pupils, Fannie Farmer.

Mary Lincoln's recipe for fish chowder is classical in its content and proportions. It begins in the fish market and carries through to the tureen. Its carefully spelled-out instructions reveal the importance attached to the dish by New Englanders. Some detailing can be ignored, such as the soaking, parboiling, and draining of the potatoes, a precaution resulting from the long-held conviction that potatoes had to be purged of poisonous content.

Whether used or not, this excellent recipe should be read as a knowledgeable essay on fish chowder. Even the seasonings suggested in the last paragraph should be noted, for they provide variations that might please habitual chowder eaters. The recipe makes eight to ten servings.

4 or 5 pounds cod or haddock or bass	1 tablespoonful salt
6 potatoes	½ teaspoonful white pepper
A 2-inch cube of fat salt pork	1 tablespoonful butter
2 small onions	1 quart milk
	6 butter crackers

When buying a fish for a chowder, have the head left on, but the skin removed . . . . Then begin at the tail and cut the fish from

From Mary J. Lincoln, *Mrs. Lincoln's Boston Cook Book* (Boston: Roberts Brothers, 1884), pp. 155–56.

the bone on one side, keeping the knife as close as possible to the bone, remove the bone from the other side. Do not forget to take out the small bones near the head. Wipe the fish carefully with a damp cloth, cut it into pieces about two inches square, and put it away in a cool place. Break the bones and head, cover with cold water, and put them on to boil. Pare and slice the potatoes one eighth of an inch thick, using enough to make the same quantity by measurement as you have of fish. Soak them in cold water half an hour, and parboil or scald in boiling water five minutes; then pour off the water. Cut the pork into quarter-inch dice, and fry it in an omelet pan. Cut the onions into thin slices and fry them in the pork fat, being careful that it does not burn. Pour the fat through a strainer into the kettle, leaving the pork scraps and onions in the strainer. Put the sliced potatoes into the kettle; hold the strainer over the potatoes, and pour through it enough boiling water to cover them. This is easier than to fry in the kettle, and skim out the pork and onions,—which to a novice would be running the risk of burning the fat, cleaning the kettle, and beginning again. When the potatoes have boiled ten minutes, strain the water in which the bones were boiled, and pour it into the kettle. Add the salt and pepper, and when the chowder is boiling briskly, put in the fish, and set it back where it can simmer ten minutes. Do not break the fish by stirring it. Add the butter and the hot milk. Split the crackers, put them in the tureen, and pour the chowder over them. Do not soak the crackers in cold water. Butter crackers will soften easily in the hot chowder. If you wish the broth thicker, stir in one cup of fine cracker crumbs, or one tablespoonful of flour cooked in one tablespoonful of butter. More milk and a little more seasoning may be added to this amount of fish and potato, if you wish to make a larger quantity. When wanted richer, beat *two eggs*, mix them with the hot milk, and put in the tureen before turning in the chowder. If added while the chowder is in the hot kettle, the eggs

will curdle. Any firm white fish may be used for a chowder, but cod and haddock are best. Many use a cod's head with the haddock. The head is rich and gelatinous, and it should always be boiled with the bones, and the liquor added to the chowder. In this chowder you have nothing but what the most dainty person may relish. There are no bones, skin, or scraps of boiled pork. Fish, potatoes, and crackers are all distinct in the creamy liquid, instead of being a pasty mush, such as is often served. For a change, the crackers may be buttered and browned.

If a highly seasoned dish be desired, boil an onion, cut into thin slices, with the potatoes; add more pepper, and either cayenne pepper, Worcestershire sauce, or curry powder. Omit the boiling water, and use only that in which the bones were boiled, when making a smaller quantity.

Mary J. Lincoln's Corn Chowder, 1884

It is not surprising that corn chowders should have appeared, for that grain had held an important place in the American diet from the time of the earliest settlements. Corn chowders had probably existed long before this one without being acknowledged in print.

This particular chowder is excellent. As in any other corn chowder, it is important to include the water used for cooking the corn. The potatoes are best sliced quite thin, but there is no need to soak and scald them. And do not forget to add a pinch or two of baking soda before the milk and tomatoes are combined. Serves eight.

1 quart raw sweet corn	1 saltspoonful white pepper
1 pint sliced potatoes	1 large tablespoonful butter
A 2-inch cube fat salt pork	1 pint sliced tomatoes
1 onion	1 pint milk
1 teaspoonful salt	6 crisped crackers

Scrape the raw corn from the cob. Boil the cobs twenty minutes in water enough to cover them; then skim them out. Pare, soak, and scald the potatoes. Fry the onion in the salt pork fat, and strain the fat into the kettle with the corn water. Add the potatoes, corn, [tomatoes,] salt, and pepper. Simmer fifteen minutes, or till the potatoes and corn are tender. Add the butter and milk, and serve very hot with crisped crackers.

From Mary J. Lincoln, *Mrs. Lincoln's Boston Cook Book* (Boston: Roberts Brothers, 1884), p. 157.

A Corn Chowder of Jules Harder, 1885

Before becoming the famous chef de cuisine *of San Francisco's magnificent Palace Hotel, Jules Harder had been at the Grand Union Hotel in Saratoga, the Union Club in New York City, and Delmonico's. His corn chowder recipe is clearly intended more for a restaurant than for a family. To make six servings, reduce the amounts to ¼ pound salt pork (or 3 slices of bacon), 1 onion, a quart of water, 3 potatoes, an equal amount of fresh corn (cream-style canned corn also works well), about 6 common crackers or 8 soda crackers, and a cup of hot milk. The directions, if followed carefully, produce an outstanding corn chowder, so delicately flavored that to add paprika or to garnish with parsley would be indecent.*

Cut one pound of fat pork in small pieces, and put them in a saucepan. When they are nicely fried remove the pieces and put four finely sliced onions in the hot fat. When they are fried, add one gallon of hot water, letting it boil until the onions are thoroughly cooked, when you will rub it through a fine sieve. Then peel one dozen potatoes, slice them fine, and cut the same quantity of green corn from the cob. Put them in a saucepan, in layers, sprinkle each layer lightly with flour, and season with salt and pepper. Then pour the above strained broth over the layers, cover the saucepan and set on the fire to boil for thirty minutes. By this time the corn and potatoes should be cooked. Then add one quart of boiled milk, a piece of butter and some crackers, split in half and soaked in cold water. Put the cover on the saucepan and cook the chowder ten minutes longer.

From Jules Arthur Harder, *The Physiology of Taste: Harder's Book of Practical American Cookery* (San Francisco, n.p., 1885), p. 128.

A Philadelphia Fish Chowder
of Sarah T. Rorer, 1886

In 1878 Sarah Tyson Rorer and four cousins founded the Philadel-
phia Cooking School; eight years later Mrs. Rorer's Philadelphia
Cook Book *won considerable acclaim. This work and Mrs.*
Lincoln's Boston Cook Book, *published in 1884, were the first to*
follow what soon became a standard cookbook format, in which
recipes contained clear step-by-step instructions and a separate list
of ingredients and quantities.

If dried herbs are used in this chowder, reduce the amounts of
thyme and marjoram to one-third those asked. And add a pinch or
two of baking soda to the chowder before adding the milk. Serves
eight.

3 pounds of fish	¼ pound of bacon or ham
1 pint of milk	1 tablespoonful of thyme
3 medium-sized potatoes	1 teaspoonful of sweet
1 quart of water	marjoram
1 pint of stewed or canned	6 water crackers or three sea
tomatoes	biscuit
1 large-sized onion	Salt and pepper to taste

Cut the fish, the potatoes, the onion, and the bacon or ham, into
pieces about a half-inch square. Now put the bacon or ham and the
onion into a frying-pan, stir and fry them a light brown. Put a layer
of the potatoes in a saucepan, then a layer of fish, then a sprinkling
of onions and bacon or ham, then a layer of tomatoes, then a

From Mrs. S. T. Rorer, *Mrs. Rorer's Philadelphia Cook Book* (Philadelphia:
Arnold and Co., [1886]), pp. 35–36.

sprinkling of thyme and sweet marjoram, salt and pepper, and continue these alternations until all is in, having the last layer potatoes. Now add the water. Cover closely, place it over a moderate fire and let it *simmer* twenty minutes without stirring. In the meantime put the milk in a farina boiler and break into it the crackers; let it stand three minutes. Now add this to the chowder, stir, let it boil once, see that it is properly seasoned and serve very hot.

The tomatoes may be omitted if not liked.

A Pennsylvania Corn Chowder, 1886

This is an excellent corn chowder, but one so thick that it is best to increase the amounts of milk and water. The recipe makes from ten to twelve servings, but the ingredients are easily cut in half for a smaller gathering.

1 quart of grated corn	3 tablespoonfuls of flour
4 good-sized potatoes	1 pint of milk
2 medium-sized onions	6 water crackers
½ pound of bacon or ham	Yolk of one egg
1 large tablespoonful of butter	½ pint of boiling water

Pare and cut the potatoes and onions into dice. Cut the bacon or ham into small pieces and put it into a frying-pan with the onions and fry until a nice brown. Put a layer of potatoes in the bottom of a saucepan, then a sprinkling of bacon or ham and onion, then a layer of corn, then a sprinkling of salt and pepper, then a layer of potatoes, and so on, until all is in, having the last layer corn. Now add the water and place over a very moderate fire and *simmer* for twenty minutes. Then add the milk. Rub the butter and flour together and stir into the boiling chowder. Add the crackers, broken; stir, and cook five minutes longer. Taste to see if properly seasoned, take it from the fire, add the beaten yolk of the egg and serve.

From Mrs. S. T. Rorer, *Mrs. Rorer's Philadelphia Cook Book* (Philadelphia: Arnold and Co., [1886]), p. 35.

A Philadelphia Potato Chowder, 1886

It is quite possible that potato chowder—easy, simple, and economical—was far more generally eaten than its relatively rare appearances in cookbooks would suggest. This fine recipe makes a tastier dish than the Nantucket potato chowder of 1874, although there may be some who prefer to increase the amounts of onion and parsley. Serves six.

6 good-sized potatoes	1 tablespoonful of chopped
1 tablespoonful of flour	parsley
1 good-sized onion	1 tablespoonful of butter
¼ pound of bacon or ham	1 pint of milk
1 pint of water	

Pare and cut the potatoes into dice and chop the onion fine. Cut the bacon or ham into small pieces. Put the bacon or ham and the onion in a frying-pan and fry until a light brown. Now put a layer of potatoes in the bottom of a saucepan, then a sprinkling of the ham or bacon, onion, parsley, salt and pepper, then a layer of potatoes, and so on until all is used. Add the water, cover closely and *simmer* twenty minutes. Then add the milk. Rub the butter and flour together, add to the boiling chowder and stir carefully until it boils. Taste to see if properly seasoned; if not, add more salt and pepper and serve.

From Mrs. S. T. Rorer, *Mrs. Rorer's Philadelphia Cook Book* (Philadelphia: Arnold and Co., [1886]), pp. 35–36. In far-off San Francisco, in 1910, Mrs. Dewey Coffin made this recipe her contribution to the *Corona Club Cook Book* (San Francisco, 1910), p. 27.

A Shaker Bean Chowder, ca. 1890

The following recipe makes a good, hearty, and easy-to-prepare chowder, though many will prefer, like this editor, to cut the salt pork in half or to substitute a few slices of bacon. Dried white beans might soak enough in six hours, but they also might not—an overnight soaking is a better bet.

1 pint dried white beans
½ pound salt pork, diced
2 onions, diced
1 quart canned tomatoes with
   juice

¼ teaspoon pepper
2 teaspoons salt
2 tablespoons molasses or
   brown sugar

Soak beans overnight or for at least 6 hours in water to cover. Fry the salt pork and onions together until the onions are somewhat soft and the pork is beginning to brown. Bring the beans to a boil, add the fried pork and onions, and then simmer gently. Continue to cook until beans are tender (approximately 30 minutes), adding water as necessary. Add tomatoes and seasonings, including the molasses or brown sugar. Simmer 30 minutes longer. Put part of the beans through a sieve to give a smooth base to the chowder. Dried split peas can be used in a similar way, with or without the tomatoes. Serves 4–6.

A "Red" Fish Chowder
of Southern Massachusetts, 1891

This first-rate chowder was contributed by Mrs. J. M. Cheney to a cookbook compiled by the Ladies Auxiliary of the Y.M.C.A. of Southbridge, Massachusetts. Like its equally delicious predecessor of 1851 it contains both milk and tomatoes. It was tested to make two servings with a pound of fish, a medium-sized potato, a small onion, 3 slices of bacon cut small, a medium-sized tomato peeled and diced, and ¾ cup of milk thickened with crumbled soda crackers. Do not forget to add a pinch of baking soda before combining the milk and tomato.

Cut a medium sized shad or white-fish, three or four potatoes, one onion, and a quarter of a pound of bacon, into small pieces. Fry the bacon and onions a light brown. Put a layer of potatoes in the sauce-pan, over that a layer of the fish, then a sprinkle of onions and bacon, then a layer of tomatoes; sprinkle with pepper and salt, alternating the layers until all is in. Add enough water to cover, place over a moderate fire and let simmer twenty-five minutes. Boil one pint of milk, thickening it with cracker crumbs; let it stand a moment and then add to the chowder. Now stir for the last time, let boil an instant, season, if not strong, to taste, and serve hot.

From *The Practical Cook. A Collection of Tested Recipes, Contributed by the Ladies Auxiliary of the Y.M.C.A. Southbridge, Mass.* (Southbridge: Journal Steam Book Print, 1891), p. 10.

Maria Parloa's Salt Codfish Chowder, 1893

Maria Parloa was pastry cook at various New Hampshire resort hotels during the 1860s and 1870s and later conducted cooking schools and wrote cookbooks. Her recipe for salt codfish chowder recognized a dish that for several centuries pleased innumerable Americans.

Several necessary injunctions: note the instructions for soaking salt cod in the "Suggestions for Chowder Making" near the front of this book; do not add any salt until the chowder is virtually completed and has been tasted; and remember not to boil, or even simmer, the chowder after the codfish has been added. Also, more than a gill (½ cup) of water may be needed to add to the pork, onion, and flour as indicated. The recipe makes two hearty servings.

1 pint of milk.	¼ teaspoonful of pepper.
½ pint of shredded codfish.	1 tablespoonful of flour.
3 gills of potato cubes.	Salt.
3 ounces of salt pork.	3 Boston crackers.
2 tablespoonfuls of minced onion.	

Wash the fish and cut it into two-inch lengths. Tear these in pieces, and, covering with cold water, soak for three or four hours. Slice the pork, and cook in the frying-pan for ten minutes. Add the onion and cook for ten minutes. Now add the flour, and stir until smooth; after which, stir in one gill of water. Put the potatoes in a stew-pan and pour the mixture in the frying-pan over them. Season with the

From Maria Parloa, *Miss Parloa's Young Housekeeper* (Boston: Estes and Lauriat, 1897), p. 95. This work was copyrighted in 1893.

pepper and half a teaspoonful of salt. Place on the fire and cook for ten minutes; then take out the slices of pork and add the fish, milk, and the crackers split. Cook gently for half an hour, being careful to let the chowder only bubble at one side of the stewpan. At the end of the half-hour, taste before serving, to be sure to have it salt enough.

Charles Ranhofer's Chowder of Freshwater Fish, 1894

The great chef of Delmonico's, Charles Ranhofer, was born in 1836 in St. Denis, France, to a family of noted cooks. Beginning at the age of twelve he worked in various French restaurants before emigrating to America where he cooked in New York City for the Russian consul, in Washington for a famous host, and for two outstanding Creole restaurants in New Orleans. Returning to France he managed a series of great balls for Napoleon III. In the early 1860s he went back to New York City, where he managed the Maison Doree, for a time Delmonico's only rival as a great restaurant, before being given complete control over Delmonico's kitchens, a post he held from 1862 until 1898.

Ranhofer named the following dish a Chowder de Poisson d'Eau Douce a la Stebens. The identity of Stebens is not given. The green peppers give the chowder a unique flavor and a greenish hue. The chowder is good whether made with saltwater fish or freshwater fish.

Prepare a pound and a half of fresh water fish, such as sole, pike, perch or wall-eyed perch (*sandre*), and cut in one and a half inch squares; also one pound of potatoes cut in half inch dice, three-quarters of a pound of minced onions, half a pound of chopped fat pork, and three green peppers chopped fine. Melt the pork, add to it the onions and the peppers, fry without coloring, then add the squares of potatoes and the fish, moisten to the height of the fish with water, season with salt and black pepper and let boil until the

From Charles Ranhofer, *The Epicurean* (New York: R. Ranhofer, 1908), p. 267. This was first published in 1894.

potatoes are cooked. This chowder must be thick and appear more like a stew, still, some broth can be added to it, to thin it out according to taste.

A Shaker Corn Chowder, ca. 1900

It was in the Shaker Village of Hancock, Massachusetts that this straightforward, simple, but very good corn chowder was made. It will have more of a chowder consistency if the stock, milk, and cream are each reduced by about a fourth. Use white, rather than black, pepper.

4 tablespoons diced salt pork	2 cups corn scraped from the
1 tablespoon butter	cob, *or* 2 cups home canned
1 medium onion, sliced	corn (called homestyle)
3 potatoes, peeled and finely	4 cups whole milk
diced	Salt and pepper
2 cups chicken stock	1 cup heavy cream

3 tablespoons butter

Fry the pork in butter, remove pieces when crispy and reserve. Add onions to fat and saute until golden. Add potatoes and stock and cook slowly until soft. Add corn and milk, lower heat, and simmer until corn is tender. Young corn takes 5 minutes. (Dried corn which has been freshened will take longer.) Add salt and pepper. Bring to a boil and remove from heat. Add cream and butter. Stir up well and pour into soup plates or tureen. Float pork on top. Serves 6.

Reprinted with permission of Macmillan Publishing Co., Inc. from *The Best of Shaker Cooking*, by Amy Bess Williams Miller and Persis Wellington Fuller. Copyright © 1970 by Shaker Community, Inc.

A Fulton Market Clam Chowder, 1902

This is a strange and well-spiced chowder. Should whole allspice and cloves not be available, a few pinches of each in ground form will do. There is no need to cook the chowder for four hours as the recipe asks; half an hour is quite enough. Serves eight.

Fry one-half pound of fat salt pork until the fat is extracted. Skim out the scraps and put in an onion chopped fine and fry it a light yellow. Turn the contents of the frying pan into a pot. Add a cupful of the strained liquor of the clams and the same quantity of water, which should have been heated together to the boiling point. Put in one quart of tomatoes stewed, the hard portions chopped. Put one-half dozen whole allspice and the same number of whole cloves into a piece of cheesecloth, tie securely, and drop into the soup. Cook four hours. Half an hour before serving add the hard part of the clams, which should have been chopped very fine, and ten minutes before the soup is to be put into the tureen add the soft part of the clams. Season with a dash of red pepper and a teaspoonful of Worcestershire sauce. This recipe is for fifty clams.

From Margaret Compton, *Grand Union Cook Book* (New York: Grand Union Tea Co., 1902), pp. 51–52.

Sarah T. Rorer's
Philadelphia Clam Chowder, 1902

A prototype of this recipe, published in 1886 in Mrs. Rorer's Philadelphia Cook Book, included a pound of veal but no white stock or onion. The earlier recipe also advised that the tomatoes, "if not liked," could be omitted.

Several suggestions might be offered: include a pinch or two of baking soda before the milk is added to prevent curdling; if dried marjoram is used, a third of a teaspoon will be adequate; and do not add the chopped clams until the last few minutes before serving. If canned clams are used, two and a half eight-ounce cans would be a rough equivalent. Makes about twelve servings.

50 clams	1 quart of white stock
½ pound of bacon	6 water crackers or 3 sea
1 pint of milk	biscuits
1 teaspoonful of powdered thyme	1 teaspoonful of sweet marjoram
1 tablespoonful of chopped parsley	1 tablespoonful of chopped onion
1 pint of stewed or canned tomatoes	3 medium sized potatoes
	1 level teaspoonful of salt

1 saltspoonful of pepper

Cut the bacon into very thin slices; put it into the bottom of a good-sized saucepan. Pare and cut the potatoes into dice. Chop the clams, and roll the crackers. Put a layer of potatoes on top of the

From Sarah Tyson Rorer, *Mrs. Rorer's New Cook Book* (Philadelphia: Arnold and Co., 1902), p. 92.

bacon; then a sprinkling of onion, thyme, sweet marjoram, parsley, salt and the tomatoes chopped; then a layer of the chopped clams; and continue the alternations until all of the materials have been used. Add the stock, which should barely cover the whole. Cover the saucepan; place it over a very slow fire and simmer for a half hour without stirring. While this is cooking, add the rolled crackers to the milk; then add them to the chowder. Cover; cook for ten minutes; stir the mixture carefully, and serve at once.

A Corn Chowder, Los Angeles, 1903

Los Angeles in 1903 contained people from all parts of the country, and it is impossible to tell where this very simple recipe for an outstanding corn chowder originated. In making it, use small to medium-sized potatoes, cook the onions in butter for about ten minutes, and add salt and white pepper to taste. Placing the corn cobs in the milk while it is heating will enhance the flavor of the chowder. The recipe makes about twelve servings, but it can be easily revised to serve four or six.

Put six onions chopped fine in porcelain kettle with one cup butter. Cook until tender, then add six ears of corn cut from the cob, six potatoes pared and sliced, six crackers and two quarts water; let all boil till potatoes are done. Put one quart milk in separate dish to boil and add last thing. Let all boil up once and serve. Do not stir while cooking, as it spoils the looks. In winter canned corn will do.

From Charles F. Lummis, *The Landmarks Club Cook Book* (Los Angeles: Out West Co., 1903), p. 23.

Fannie Farmer's Fish Chowder, 1906

Except for a few words added to clarify one sentence, this recipe is that which appeared in Fannie Farmer's first edition of 1896. Notice that the solid parts of both onions and pork are discarded in this fine, rich chowder; this may have followed the dictates of Victorian delicacy. As given, the recipe makes about ten servings, but the quantities are easily halved. Note that the ''4 lb.'' refers to a whole fish.

4 lb. cod or haddock	1 ½ inch cube fat salt pork
6 cups potatoes cut in ¼ inch slices, or 4 cups potatoes cut in ¾ inch cubes	1 tablespoon salt
	1/8 teaspoon pepper
	3 tablespoons butter
1 sliced onion	4 cups scalded milk

8 common crackers

Order the fish skinned, but head and tail left on. Cut off head and tail and remove fish from backbone. Cut fish in two-inch pieces and set aside. Put head, tail, and backbone broken in pieces, in stewpan; add two cups cold water and bring slowly to boiling point; cook twenty minutes. Cut salt pork in small pieces and try out, add onion, and fry five minutes; strain fat into stewpan. Parboil potatoes five minutes in boiling water to cover; drain, and add potatoes to fat; then add two cups boiling water and cook five minutes. Add liquor drained from bones, then add the fish; cover, and simmer ten minutes. Add milk, salt, pepper, butter, and crackers split and soaked in enough cold milk to moisten. Pilot bread is sometimes used in place of common crackers.

From Fannie Merritt Farmer, *The Boston Cooking-School Cook Book* (Boston: Little, Brown & Co., 1906), pp. 127–28.

Fannie Farmer's
Connecticut Fish Chowder, 1906

Like the preceding recipe, upon which it depends for much of its instructions, this Connecticut chowder had been given in the 1896 edition. This variety—as do those that use both milk and tomatoes —offers a most pleasant meal to all who are addicted to chowders but are not steeped in prejudice.

4 lb. cod or haddock
4 cups potatoes cut in ¾ -inch
   cubes
1 ½ -inch cube fat salt pork
1 sliced onion

2 ½ cups stewed and strained
   tomatoes
3 tablespoons butter
⅔ cup cracker crumbs
Salt and pepper

Prepare same as Fish Chowder, using liquor drained from bones for cooking potatoes, instead of additional water. Use tomatoes in place of milk and add cracker crumbs just before serving.

From Fannie Merritt Farmer, *The Boston Cooking-School Cook Book* (Boston: Little, Brown & Co., 1906), p. 128.

Fannie Farmer's Clam Chowder, 1906

Here is a classic Boston clam chowder. If common crackers are not available, soda crackers can be used—in which case no soaking in milk is needed. The chowder is quite liquid, and some will wish to reduce the milk and water partially.

1 quart clams [36 soft-shell]	1 tablespoon salt
4 cups potatoes cut in ¾ inch dice	1/8 teaspoon pepper
1 ½ inch cube fat salt pork	4 tablespoons butter
1 sliced onion	4 cups scalded milk
	8 common crackers

Clean and pick over clams, using one cup cold water; drain, reserve liquor, heat to boiling point, and strain. Chop finely hard part of clams; cut pork in small pieces and try out; add onion, fry five minutes, and strain into a stewpan. Parboil potatoes five minutes in boiling water to cover; drain and put a layer in bottom of stewpan, add chopped clams, sprinkle with salt and pepper, and dredge generously with flour; add remaining potatoes, again sprinkle with salt and pepper, dredge with flour, and add two and one-half cups boiling water. Cook ten minutes, add milk, soft part of clams, and butter; boil three minutes, and add crackers split and soaked in enough cold milk to moisten. Reheat clam water to boiling point, and thicken with one tablespoon butter and flour cooked together. Add to chowder just before serving.

The clam water has a tendency to cause the milk to separate, hence is added at the last.

From Fannie Merritt Farmer, *The Boston Cooking-School Cook Book* (Boston: Little, Brown & Co., 1906), pp. 128–29.

Alexander Filippini's Oyster Chowder, 1906

Alexander Filippini served as a cook at Delmonico's restaurant and moved upward, or rather outward, to become manager of the lower Broadway branch of that establishment. When that branch was closed in the late 1880s, Filippini became a successful compiler of cookbooks and adviser on food to railway and steamship lines. In 1902 he made a worldwide tour of inspection, largely culinary it would seem, for the International Mercantile Marine Company. Four years later his International Cook Book *was published. Despite his travels, Filippini's Oyster Chowder bears the mark of New York, for the substitution of clams for oysters would make it kin to a Manhattan clam chowder. The recipe makes eight to ten servings.*

Cut in small square pieces two leeks and two medium white onions, place in a saucepan with two ounces salt pork cut in small squares, add one tablespoon melted butter, gently brown for six minutes, frequently stirring meanwhile. Pour in two quarts water and let boil for twenty minutes, cut three medium, peeled, raw potatoes into third-of-an-inch squares, add to the soup with three fresh, peeled, crushed, red tomatoes. Season with two teaspoons salt, two table-spoons Worcestershire sauce, two tablespoons tomato catsup, six drops tabasco and two saltspoons shredded dried thyme, mix well and slowly cook for forty-five minutes. Open thirty-six medium, fresh oysters. Cut them in four pieces each and add to the soup with their own liquor, then boil for ten minutes. Pour the chowder into a soup tureen, sprinkle half a teaspoon freshly chopped parsley over, place six broken soda crackers over the chowder and serve.

From Alexander Filippini, *The International Cook Book* (Garden City, N.Y.: Doubleday, Page & Co., 1913), pp. 737–38. This work was copyrighted in 1906.

A Clam Chowder of Joe Tilden, San Francisco, 1907

This recipe of a renowned amateur cook does no harm to San Francisco's reputation as a center of culinary excellence. The inclusion of green peppers was, for the time, a typical California touch. The dish will need some white pepper and some salt, though the latter should be added with care if fresh clams are used. It might also be well to add the clams not more than five minutes before the chowder is to be served.

Have one hundred clams still in the shell. Boil them in a quart of water until the shells open. Take the clams out of the kettle, saving the water in which they were boiled. Remove them from the shells, discarding all but the soft part. Take six slices of salt pork and cut into dice. Fry until crisp and a light brown. Remove from the saucepan and in the fat fry four onions sliced. Then add the water strained from the clams and the fried pork. To this add six potatoes cut in small pieces and two green peppers chopped or finely sliced. Boil the mixture fifteen minutes before putting in the clams and four sea biscuits, broken into pieces. Then boil for fifteen minutes longer and add a quart of milk. Have half a cup of bread crumbs rubbed into four ounces of butter. Stir this in as the chowder heats after the milk has been added. When it boils, it is ready to serve.

From *Joe Tilden's Recipes for Epicures* (San Francisco: A. M. Robertson, 1907), pp. 12–13.

Force Meat Balls for Chowder, San Francisco, 1907

These are excellent tidbits that are easily made and add a new dimension to any seafood chowder. They can be made in quantity and frozen for future use.

Take the meat of a good sized crab, a tumblerful of shrimps and a clove of garlic. Chop all very fine and make into small force meat balls with a beaten egg. Fry them a light brown in butter, and serve in any fish chowder or soup.

From *Joe Tilden's Recipes for Epicures* (San Francisco: A. M. Robertson, 1907), p. 13.

"Scott's" Fish Chowder, San Francisco, 1907

With a pound of fish, 2 medium-sized onions, 2 large tomatoes, a large potato, 8 common crackers, salt and pepper, and ¾ cup Bordeaux, this will turn out a very good chowder for four. Three slices of bacon can be substituted for the salt pork.

Cover the bottom of a deep pot with slices of pork cut very thin. Add a layer of fish sliced and seasoned with salt and pepper, a layer of onions parboiled and quartered, a layer of tomatoes sliced and seasoned, a layer of thickly sliced potatoes and a layer of broken sea biscuit. Repeat the layers until the pot is filled. Just cover the fish with water and cook one hour very slowly. Add one pint of claret, cook one-half hour longer and serve.

From *Joe Tilden's Recipes for Epicures* (San Francisco: A. M. Robertson, 1907), p. 10.

90

A Creole Fish Chowder, New Orleans, 1916

The six generous servings provided by this recipe are so thick that the addition of a little water or stock may be needed. Do not add milk. If the potatoes are sliced thin, only fifteen minutes may be needed for cooking after the fish, tomatoes, and potatoes are added. A quarter teaspoon of dried thyme may be sufficient for those who do not have it fresh, and one dried bay leaf should be adequate.

> 2 Pounds of Fresh Fish, Preferably Redfish or Sheepshead.
> 3 Medium-Sized Potatoes. 1 Onion. 1 Clove of Garlic.
> 3 Sprigs Each of Thyme, Parsley and Bay Leaf.
> ½ Can of Tomatoes. ½ Cup of Milk. 1 Quart of Boiling Water.
> 2 Ounces of Salt Pork or Ham Chopped Very Fine.
> Grated Oyster Crackers.
> Salt, Cayenne and Black Pepper to Taste.

Cut two pounds of fresh fish of any kind, preferably the Redfish or Sheepshead. Take three medium-sized potatoes and one onion and cut into slices. Take two ounces of salt pork, wash well and chop very fine. Put the pork into a frying pan, and when it is hot add the sliced onion. Smother slightly, and add chopped thyme, parsley, bay leaf, one clove of garlic, very fine, and Cayenne and black pepper to taste. Let this simmer for about ten minutes longer. Pour over this one quart of boiling water, and add fish and half a can of tomatoes and the potatoes. Season to taste, and cover the pan and

From *The Picayune Creole Cook Book*, 5th ed. (New Orleans: The Times-Picayune, 1916), p. 30.

91

let the contents simmer for half an hour. A half cup of milk may be added, if desired. Take oyster crackers, place in a bowl and pour the chowder over and serve hot.

A San Francisco Clam Chowder, 1919

Franz Hirtzler, former chef of the St. Francis Hotel in San Francisco, offered this second cousin to the Manhattan clam chowder. A more chowder-like consistency will result if the stock or fish broth is reduced by a third. Should dried thyme be used, cut the amount to a third. This recipe serves from twelve to sixteen people, depending on the amount of stock used, but the ingredients can be easily halved or quartered.

Chop two onions, one leek, a piece of celery and one green onion in small pieces, also cut one-half pound of salt pork in small squares. Put all together in a vessel with two ounces of butter and simmer till well done. Then add one gallon of stock or fish broth, four potatoes cut in half inch squares, salt, pepper, a little paprika, one teaspoonful of sugar, one teaspoonful of chopped thyme, a little chopped parsley, and four peeled tomatoes cut in small dices; or chopped canned tomatoes. Bring to a boil and let cook for about one hour. Put one hundred well-washed Little Neck clams in a separate vessel and put on fire with one-half glass of water and boil for ten minutes. Strain the broth and add to the chowder. Remove the clams from the shells, cut in four pieces and add to the chowder with one cup of cracker meal, and boil for four minutes. Serve with broken crackers.

From Victor Hirtzler, *The Hotel St. Francis Cook Book* (Chicago: The Hotel Monthly Press, [1919]), p. 363.

"Grandmother's Parsnip Chowder," 1920

This outstanding vegetable chowder from Worcester, Massachusetts is improved by several changes. Increase the cubed parsnips to 2½ cups, reduce the cubed potatoes to 1 cup, use just enough water to cover, and instead of a quart of milk use 1½ cups of whole milk and 1 cup of light cream. The pork, onion, butter, and cracker crumbs can remain as they are, but add salt and white pepper to taste. Dice the potatoes and parsnips quite small. As modified, this recipe will make six large servings.

3 slices fat salt pork, diced	1 quart scalded milk
1 medium-sized onion sliced thin	3 tablespoonfuls butter
2 cupfuls cubed raw potato	4 water crackers, or ½ cupful cracker-crumbs
1 ½ cupfuls cubed raw parsnips	2 teaspoonfuls salt
3 cupfuls boiling water	¼ teaspoonful pepper

Combine the salt pork and onion in the soup-kettle and cook for five minutes, taking care not to burn the onion; add to this half of the potatoes, the parsnips, and the remaining potatoes, sprinkle over the salt and pepper, add the boiling water, and simmer until the vegetables are soft. Then add the scalded milk, butter, and crackers split and soaked in cold milk, or the crumbs.

From *Good Housekeeping's Book of Recipes and Household Discoveries* (New York: Good Housekeeping Magazine, 1920), p. 156.

A New England Fish Chowder, 1926

In 1923 the Boston Herald-Traveler began a test-kitchen in the heart of Boston's shopping district, and in time published some of the recipes worked out there. It took a brave newspaper to risk its reputation with a fish chowder in Boston, but the following recipe could have increased the paper's circulation.

The salt pork is important to the flavor of this chowder, but many will choose to fry it crisp rather than to stew it with the other ingredients, if only for the sake of the texture.

Put into a large kettle one cup of broth made from the bones and head of haddock or codfish. Add one thinly sliced onion, one pound of fish sprinkled with a mixture of one teaspoon of salt, one eighth teaspoon of black pepper, pinch of ground mace and a speck of cayenne. Add one cup of solid oysters, two tablespoons of butter or margarine, either melted or cut into bits, and one fourth pound of Boston crackers. Over these place in succession another pound of fish sprinkled with the same seasonings in the same amounts as before, then oysters, fat and crackers. Lay over all one fourth pound of salt pork sliced paper thin. Cover the pot closely and let it stew for half an hour, adding more water if the mixture gets too dry. Before serving pour over the whole one half to one cup of thin cream, first heated. This will make eight servings.

From Marjorie Mills, *Better Homes Recipe Book* (Boston: Herald-Traveler, [1926]), p. 76.

A Lima Bean Chowder, 1927

Should it be necessary to make this fine chowder with dried lima beans, soak them overnight and then cook them until nearly done, retaining the water they were cooked in for the chowder. A table-spoon of chopped parsley is a nice addition. Two cups of lima beans are recommended as are three carrots. In place of the pint of hot milk with flour and fat thickening, a thin, flavored cream sauce is suggested. See page 21.

1 good slice pork	Salt
2 onions minced	Pepper
4 potatoes	1 pint hot milk
2 or 3 new carrots	1 tablespoonful flour
1 or 2 cupfuls fresh lima beans	1 tablespoonful fat

Dice the pork and fry in the kettle in which the chowder is to be made. Add the onions minced and cook in the fat until a very light brown, then add the potatoes cut in small cubes, the carrots sliced, the lima beans, and salt and pepper to taste. Cover with boiling water and simmer, covered, until all are tender. Then add the hot milk. Thicken slightly with the fat and flour blended together. Serves four or five.

From *Good Housekeeping's Book of Good Meals*, 9th ed. (New York: Good Housekeeping, 1929), p. 129. This was copyrighted in 1927.

A Corn Chowder Bisque, 1927

This hearty corn chowder can be made with canned ''home style'' or creamed corn when fresh corn is unavailable. For a richer chowder, replace part of the milk with some light cream. A sprinkling of parsley on each serving is a nice touch.

2 slices salt pork	¼ teaspoonful pepper
4 small onions	6 ears corn
6 medium potatoes	¼ teaspoonful soda
4 medium tomatoes	1 quart hot milk
2 teaspoonfuls salt	1 tablespoonful flour
1 tablespoonful butter	

Cut the salt pork into one-quarter inch cubes, and fry until light brown and crisp in the kettle in which the chowder is to be made. Remove from the stove and add the onions finely minced, potatoes cubed or sliced, tomatoes peeled and diced, arranging them in layers. Sprinkle with salt and pepper over each layer, using two teaspoonfuls of salt and one-fourth teaspoonful of pepper in all. Cover with one pint boiling water and simmer until the vegetables are nearly tender. Then add the corn from the six ears which have been first scored down through the middle, the tips sliced off with a sharp knife, and the pulp pressed and scraped off. Cook ten minutes more, add the soda, and milk, which has been thickened slightly with the butter and flour melted together. Stir rapidly while adding the milk, and serve hot with toasted crackers and a green salad. If canned corn is used, measure two cupfuls. Serves six to eight.

From *Good Housekeeping's Book of Good Meals*, 9th ed. (New York: Good Housekeeping, 1929), pp. 128–29.

An Oyster and Mushroom Chowder, 1939

Oysters and mushrooms go together nicely in this dish. It is probably best to quarter or slice the mushrooms, unless they are very small, and to heat them in the butter until they have a pleasing texture. Serve with thin slices of buttered toast.

1 quart large oysters	½ cup cream or evaporated
1 cup oyster liquor	milk
3 tablespoons butter	2 shallots, minced
1 tablespoon flour	1 sprig parsley, minced
1 cup milk	Salt and pepper

½ pound mushrooms

Heat oysters in own liquor below boiling point until edges curl. Drain, saving the liquor. Melt 1 tablespoon butter, blend in flour, add milk gradually, stirring constantly, bring to boiling point and cook 1 minute. Add cream, shallots, parsley, salt and pepper. Heat cleaned mushrooms in the remaining butter until hot, but do not brown. Add mushrooms, oysters and oyster liquor to cream sauce, serve hot. Serves 6.

From *The United States Regional Cookbook* (Chicago: The Culinary Arts Institute, 1947), p. 172. This work appeared first in 1939.

"Great-Aunt Alice's Clam Chowder," 1941

A baked chowder! This recipe, its title hinting that it dates from the late nineteenth century, together with the English baked salmon chowder of 1830 mentioned in the introduction, suggests that there may have existed in the chowder family an obscure collateral line.

The following recipe will require a full three hours to bake in order that the potatoes and salt pork be well cooked and that the flavors fully intermingle. The end result is excellent and thoroughly different, both in taste and texture, from all other known clam chowders.

2 dozen clams	Thyme
2 medium-sized onions	Black pepper and salt
½ pound salt pork	Milk
3 large potatoes	3 large handfuls rolled crackers

Chop the clams, not too fine. Also chop the onions, very fine. Cut pork and potatoes into small dice. Put in a baking dish a layer of pork, [one of onions,] one of potatoes, one of clams, and so on. Add some of the cracker crumbs, ½ level teaspoonful thyme and black pepper and salt to taste. Cover these materials with clam liquor and milk to a depth of 1 inch above the chowder. Sprinkle with cracker crumbs. Bake for about 3 hours, or until the liquid has disappeared. Temperature about 350°F. Serves 6.

From Katharine Del Valle, *Recipes of a Rolling Stone* (New York: Coward-McCann, [1941]), pp. 68–69.

A New England Clam Chowder of Dione Lucas and Marion Gorman, 1947

Dione Lucas and Marion Gorman, both graduates of the Ecole du Cordon Bleu, *published the* Dione Lucas Book of French Cooking *in 1947. Dione Lucas also founded the famous Cordon Bleu restaurant in New York, edited other cookbooks, and in 1947 became one of the first to teach cooking on television.*

The following clam chowder is outstanding and needs not a single revision.

2 tablespoons salt butter
1 Bermuda onion, finely chopped
1 teaspoon finely chopped garlic
2 stalks celery, finely chopped
24 fresh shelled chowder clams
2 cups clam juice, fresh or canned
Salt
Freshly cracked black pepper
6 ounces salt pork, cut into small dice
2 Idaho-type potatoes, peeled and cut into small dice
2 cups light cream
4 tablespoons frozen sweet butter
1 tablespoon chopped fresh chives
1 tablespoon chopped fresh parsley
Freshly cracked white pepper
Coarse salt
3 small French rolls

Melt 1 tablespoon salt butter in a heavy pan. Add the chopped onion, garlic, and celery, and cook very slowly 4 minutes. Put the raw clams through a fine meat chopper. Add another tablespoon of salt butter to the pan, add the chopped clams, moisten with 4 tablespoons clam juice, and season with salt and black pepper. Cover and cook very slowly 10 to 15 minutes.

Blanch the salt pork in boiling water, strain, and saute in a large heavy pan until nearly crisp. Plunge the diced potatoes into boiling water for 2 minutes. Drain, dry, and add to the salt pork. Pour in the rest of the clam juice, bring slowly to a boil, and simmer gently until the potatoes are soft. Remove the pan from the heat and mix in the chopped clams. Stir in the cream and continue stirring over the heat until the chowder comes to a boil. Cut the frozen sweet butter into 4 slices, ladle the soup into individual bowls, and float a slice of frozen butter on top of each. Sprinkle chopped chives and parsley, freshly cracked black and white pepper, and a very little coarse salt into each bowl. Cut the French rolls into very thin slices lengthwise, toast them quickly under a hot broiler, and serve on a napkin. Net: 4 servings.

A Manhattan Clam Chowder, 1947

Devotees of Manhattan clam chowder will find it hard to criticize this version by Dione Lucas and Marion Gorman. A smaller quantity of caraway seeds might be desirable, and some people will enjoy a few drops of tabasco sauce in each serving.

3 ounces salt pork, cut into
  ½-inch cubes
1 large yellow onion, chopped
1 leek, washed and chopped
2 medium-size potatoes, peeled
  and cut into small cubes
4 large ripe tomatoes, skinned
  and coarsely chopped
1 stalk celery, chopped
1 green pepper, seeded and
  chopped

1 bay leaf
½ teaspoon thyme
5 cups water
12 large fresh clams, shelled,
  and the clam liquor
Salt
Freshly cracked white pepper
½ teaspoon caraway seeds
Water crackers or hot
  biscuits

Heat a large heavy pan, put in the cubed salt pork, and render a little of the fat. Put in the chopped onion and leek, and cook over moderate heat until they are lightly browned. Add the potatoes, tomatoes, celery, green pepper, bay leaf, thyme, water, and the liquor from the clams. Season with salt and pepper. Bring the mixture to a boil over moderate heat; reduce the heat and simmer gently 30 to 35 minutes, until the vegetables are tender. Cut the clams into small bits and add them to the soup. Add the caraway seeds and cook the soup 5 more minutes over low heat. Serve with water crackers or hot biscuits. Net: 6 servings.

From *The Dione Lucas Book of French Cooking*, by Dione Lucas and Marion Gorman, by permission of Little, Brown and Co. Copyright 1947 by Dione Lucas. Copyright © 1973 by Mark Lucas and Marion F. Gorman.

A Dione Lucas
Clam and Oyster Chowder, 1947

This delicious and delicately flavored chowder is easily and quickly made, once the few ingredients are gathered. Crisp crackers or crisp buttered toast, served on the side, go well with it.

2 tablespoons butter	1 dozen raw hard clams
1 tablespoon oil	3 cups light cream
1 tablespoon mixed scallion,	salt
onion, and garlic	cayenne pepper
1 dozen raw oysters	4 tablespoons butter

small handful chopped parsley

Heat butter and oil in a pan and add mixed scallion, onion, and garlic. Cook for 2 minutes; then add cut-up oysters and clams. Pour on cream and season with salt and cayenne pepper. Bring very lightly to a boil, then add bit by bit butter and parsley. Simmer a few minutes and serve.

From *The Cordon Bleu Cook Book*, by Dione Lucas, by permission of Little, Brown and Co. Copyright 1947 by Dione Lucas.

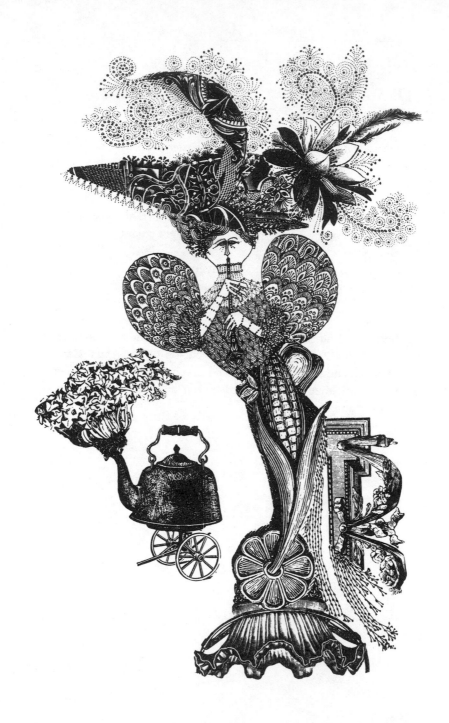

Louis P. De Gouy's Corn Chowder, 1948

Louis P. De Gouy was trained in the culinary arts by his father, "Esquire of the Cuisine" to Emperor Franz Joseph of Austria, and by the great Escoffier. The younger De Gouy was deeply interested in the use of seasonings to improve the flavor of certain dishes. His skill appears clearly in this outstanding corn chowder, best served with a crusty bread or thin slices of buttered toast. Serves four.

Brown lightly ½ cup of salt pork, cut in small dice; stir in 3 or 4 thin slices of onion, and cook 2 or 3 minutes, stirring frequently, over a gentle flame. Then add 1 small bay leaf tied with 5 or 6 sprigs of fresh parsley and 1 small sprig of thyme. Season to taste with salt, pepper and a dash of sage, then stir in 1 cup of raw potatoes, diced small, and 2 cups of hot water. Cook until the potatoes are tender. Thicken the mixture with 3 tablespoons of flour mixed smoothly with a little cold water or milk. Add 2½ cups of canned or freshly cooked whole kernel corn and 2 cups of scalded rich milk, and stir well. Bring the whole to a boil; remove from the fire and, just before serving, stir in 2 fresh egg yolks, slightly beaten, and 1 tablespoon of butter. Dust with finely chopped parsley or chives, and serve very hot.

From Louis P. De Gouy, *The Gold Cook Book* (New York: Galahad Books, 1973), p. 118. This was first published in 1948 by Chilton Book Company, and we reprint here with their permission.

De Gouy's Codfish Chowder, Newfoundland Style, 1948

One suspects that this carefully flavored chowder is more indebted to De Gouy than to Newfoundland. Those who do not insist that the fish flavor be more prominent will enjoy this recipe.

Wipe 3–3½ pounds of codfish with a damp cloth and place in a heavy soup kettle with 5 cups of cold water and ¾ teaspoon of salt, 1 bouquet garni composed of 1 large bay leaf, 8 sprigs of fresh parsley, 1 sprig of thyme, and 1 sprig of green celery leaves (top), tied together with kitchen thread, 1 whole clove, 1 blade of garlic, and 8 whole peppercorns. Bring slowly to a boil; lower the flame and simmer very gently for about 25 minutes. Strain the broth through a fine-meshed wire sieve into a soup kettle. Skin and carefully bone the fish, and set it aside to keep hot. Fry a 2¾ to 3-inch cube of salt pork fat back, cut into small cubes, add 2 medium-sized onions, thinly sliced, and add to the fish broth with 2 cups of diced small potatoes. Cook until potatoes are almost tender (about 10 minutes). Return the shredded, boned, skinned fish to the chowder; stir in 2 cups of scalded thin cream or undiluted evaporated milk; bring to a boil; taste for seasoning, and when ready to serve stir in 1 tablespoon of minced parsley and 1½ tablespoons of butter. Serve in hot plates each containing a toasted cracker.

Any kind of fresh, uncooked white-fleshed fish may be prepared in this manner.

From Louis P. De Gouy, *The Gold Cook Book* (New York: Galahad Books, 1973), p. 131. This was first published in 1948 by Chilton Book Company, and is reprinted here with their permission.

A Maine Lobster Chowder, 1948

Here is a delightful chowder that is a ''Maine'' dish only in that it uses a Maine lobster; the subtle, carefully balanced flavors are those of De Gouy. As indicated, toast—crisp and buttered—nicely complements the chowder. Serves four.

Remove the meat from a cooked 2½ pound lobster and cut in small dice. Cream 2 tablespoons of butter; add the liver of the lobster (green part), and 2 ordinary soda crackers finely rolled. Mix well. Scald 1 quart of milk with 1 cup of cream with a small slice of onion, a tiny pinch of powdered thyme, a small bay leaf, 1 whole clove, 4 crushed peppercorns, a sprig of parsley and a blade of garlic and strain over the creamed butter and lobster liver mixture, stirring occasionally while pouring slowly. Cook the crushed shells of the lobster in 1 cup of cold water for 10 minutes over a very hot flame, and strain through cheese cloth over the milk mixture. Season to taste with salt, generously with paprika and a few grains of freshly grated nutmeg, then beat in 2 egg yolks, slightly beaten with 2 tablespoons of sherry wine, stirring briskly. Last of all, stir in the diced lobster meat; heat well but do not boil, and serve with toast.

From Louis P. De Gouy, *The Gold Cook Book* (New York: Galahad Books, 1973), pp. 133–34. This was first published in 1948 by Chilton Book Company, and we reprint here with their permission.

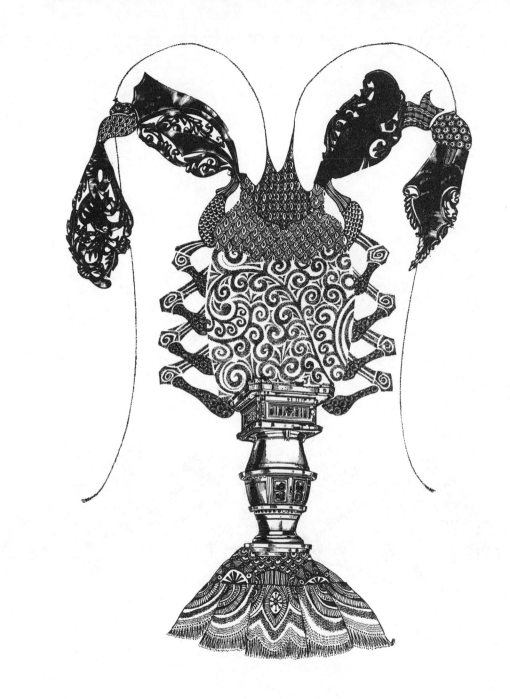

A Crabmeat and Corn Chowder, 1948

A strict definition of chowder might leave this dish outside the pale, as it omits the usual salt pork and onion basis. But while the recipe is somewhat fussy, the result is delicious, especially if a flavored white sauce (see page 21) is used. Crisp buttered toast or croutons can be substituted for the salted crackers.

Combine 2 ½ cups of fresh grated corn, or cream style canned corn, 3 thin slices of onion, 2 ½ cups of scalded sweet milk, and cook over boiling water 20–25 minutes. Take out the onion slices, if you wish, then force liquid and corn through a coarse sieve. Add to it 2 ½ cups of thin white or cream sauce and bring the whole to the boiling point. Stir in 2 beaten egg yolks, one at a time, beating briskly after each addition, and season to taste with salt, white pepper and a grating of nutmeg. Just before serving, stir in 1 cup of flaked crabmeat, either freshly cooked or canned, but carefully boned. Serve very hot with salted crackers.

From Louis P. De Gouy, *The Gold Cook Book* (New York: Galahad Books, 1973), p. 132. This was first published in 1948 by Chilton Book Company, and we reprint here with their permission.

A Canned Salmon Chowder, 1949

This is an excellent chowder that is best made with fresh salmon, of course, but may also use canned red sockeye salmon. In any case the consistency will be improved if the cream sauce is made with two, rather than three, cups of milk. Thus made, one can expect six generous servings. Crisp salted crackers are a good accompaniment.

1 lb. can salmon (2 cups)	4 tablespoons butter
2 cups water	4 tablespoons flour
1 cup tomato juice	1 teaspoon salt
½ cup diced onion	1 teaspoon dry mustard
1 cup cubed raw potatoes	3 cups milk
1 teaspoon celery salt	½ tsp. Worcestershire sauce

Clean salmon. Combine salmon, water, tomato juice, potatoes, onions and celery salt in a large kettle. Cover and simmer slowly for 30–40 minutes. In another pan make cream sauce of butter, flour and milk; add salt, mustard and Worcestershire sauce. When thick and smooth, add cream sauce to salmon mixture. Stir well and serve hot.

From the University of Chicago Settlement League, *Settlement Dough-Nations: A Recipe Book* (Chicago: Chief Printing Co., 1949), p. 7. Recipe is attributed to Elizabeth H. Woellner.

Helen Evans Brown's Abalone Chowder, 1952

Some trying abalone for the first time discover that they prefer its taste to that of clams. It is unfortunate that fresh abalone can be bought only along the California and Mexican coasts. However, stores that carry Japanese foods sell fine canned abalone, and any conscientious grocer should be willing to order some from his wholesaler.

This recipe produces a delicious, delicately flavored chowder. For the white wine, a good dry vermouth works well.

1 ½ pounds abalone	1 cup sliced onion
3 cups chicken stock	2 cups diced raw potatoes
(or salted water)	2 cups cream
1 herb bouquet	1 cup white wine
¼ pound salt pork	Salt and pepper

Minced parsley

Simmer 1 ½ pounds of abalone—whole or sliced—in 3 cups of chicken stock or salted (1 teaspoon) water, with an herb bouquet of thyme, parsley, and bay. When tender enough to pierce easily with a fork, drain, reserving the liquid, and grind the meat. Dice ¼ pound of salt pork and cook it until it's a beautiful crisp amber. Remove the pork and save, then add a cup of sliced onion to the fat, and cook it until it colors. Two cups of diced raw potatoes come next, and the abalone with its liquid is simmered with the vegetables, along with salt and pepper to taste. When the potatoes are done, 2 cups of cream (milk will do, but not as nicely) and a cup of white wine are poured in, the pork cubes are returned to the chowder, and the seasoning is corrected. The chowder is poured into a tureen and sprinkled with parsley. That's all, except for some pilot biscuits—and an appetite. Serves 6 to 8.

A Southern Louisiana Fish Chowder, 1954

Here is an excellent Creole chowder of well-considered proportions and consistency. It was tested to make two very large servings with a pound of sliced redfish; 3 cups of stock (the bouquet garni *made with a small bay leaf, 2 celery leaves, 2 parsley sprigs, and a sprig of thyme); ¼ cup each of chopped celery and chopped shallots; ¼ green pepper, chopped; a small handful of parsley; a medium-sized potato; and ⅓ cup of milk; with salt and fresh-ground black pepper to taste. Serve with bread sticks.*

Simmer four whole or sliced fish in four quarts of water for forty minutes with a *bouquet garni* until tender. Remove bones and flake the fish. Save the stock. Saute one cup of minced shallots, one cup of celery, one-half cup of parsley, and one bell pepper in olive oil for five minutes in an iron skillet. Add stock and one-half pound of thinly sliced potatoes to skillet. Simmer for twenty minutes until potatoes are tender. Add fish and one cup of hot milk; let simmer a few minutes. Serves eight.

From *Mary Land's Louisiana Cookery* (Baton Rouge, La.: Louisiana State University Press, 1954), p. 46. Reprinted by permission of the publisher.

A Cape Cod Portuguese Fish Chowder, 1954

The Portuguese have long been known for their fish cookery, and those who settled in New England fishing towns continued the tradition. This thick and hearty fish chowder is given a unique character by the use of vinegar and saffron, the latter an essential ingredient of the French bouillabaisse.

½ cup salt pork cubes
1 cup chopped onion
3 cups diced potatoes
1 teaspoon salt
¼ teaspoon pepper

½ teaspoon saffron
1 tablespoon vinegar
2 pounds lean fish (haddock, whiting or flounder) cut in chunks

In deep, heavy kettle, try out pork cubes slowly, turning occasionally, until only crisp pork bits remain. Remove these to use later. In the hot fat, fry onion slowly until soft and golden. Add 6 cups cold water, potatoes, seasonings and vinegar. Boil until potatoes are half done. Add fish. Continue cooking gently until fish is tender. Add browned bits of pork. Serves 6.

From Peter Hunt, *Cape Cod Cookbook* (New York: Hawthorn Books, 1954), pp. 20–21. Reprinted by permission of the publisher.

A Scallop Chowder, 1960

The borderline between chowders and soups can be a narrow one, and this dish approaches it. Still, it is very good and can be thickened by reducing the cream and water or by adding more butter and flour thickening. It is desirable to quarter the scallops. If the sherry is added, it should be only up to the point where the flavor is modified but the delicate taste of the scallops is still clearly present.

1 pint scallops	½ teaspoon salt
3 tablespoons flour	1/8 teaspoon pepper
¼ cup melted butter	¾ tablespoon sherry
3 cups light cream	(optional)
1 tablespoon minced onion	2 slices crisp bacon crumbled

Cook the scallops in a small amount of water and put through the food grinder. Make a cream sauce by blending the flour with 3 tablespoons butter and adding the cream slowly and the water in which the scallops were cooked. When slightly thickened, add the scallops; then add the minced onion which has been sauteed in butter. Season with salt and pepper, and add the sherry if you wish. Garnish with crumbled crisp bacon. Yield: 1 ½ quarts.

A Seafood Chowder, 1960

This is not a difficult chowder, but it does require some effort to collect the ingredients and more than an hour in the kitchen to use them. The result, though, is a first-rate dish that has both interest and depth of flavor. Some may choose to omit the curry powder; if used it should be cooked for a few minutes in the bacon fat.

1 small lobster	1 (6 ½ -ounce) can crabmeat
1 pound fresh shrimp	2 medium onions, chopped
5 cups boiling water	¼ pound bacon, diced
1 small onion	1 tablespoon curry powder
3 teaspoons salt	2 cups cream
1 bay leaf	3 cups milk
2 thick slices lemon	1 teaspoon paprika
1 pound sea scallops quartered	1/8 teaspoon white pepper
or 1 pound bay scallops	Dash hot pepper sauce
uncut	2 tablespoons butter
1 pound fillet of sole or halibut	Chopped parsley or watercress
2 cups diced potatoes	(garnish)

Put the lobster and shrimp into the boiling water with the small onion, 2 teaspoons salt, bay leaf and lemon. Simmer for 15 minutes. Remove the lobster and shrimp from the stock. Cool, shell and devein the shrimp and, if large, split lengthwise. Remove lobster meat from the shell and cut into bite-size pieces. Return shrimp shells and lobster shells to the stock and simmer together for

From *Ladies' Home Journal Cookbook*, by Carol Truax. Copyright © 1960, 1963 by The Curtis Publishing Company. Reprinted by permission of Doubleday & Company, Inc.

half an hour. Strain the stock, add the scallops, sole or halibut and potatoes, and cook for 15 minutes. Remove the fillets and flake the fish coarsely, removing any bones. Return to stock and add the picked over crabmeat. Saute the bacon and chopped onions until golden in 6-quart soup kettle. Stir in curry and 1 teaspoon salt. Add 1 quart of the fish stock, cream and milk. Add lobster meat, shrimp, fish and onions to stock. Season with paprika, white pepper and hot pepper sauce. Add the butter and heat until almost boiling. Adjust seasoning to taste. Serve from tureen or in bowls topped with chopped parsley or cress. Any kind of fish may be used; more of one shellfish may be used and another omitted. Two lobster tails will serve instead of 1 whole lobster. Yield: 3½ quarts.

Craig Claiborne's Fish Chowder, 1961

Here is a wonderful use for fishheads and bones that might other-wise be discarded after a meal; or, your fish market will probably give them to you fresh without charge. In either case, a surprising amount of flesh can be recovered, which, with the good broth, can be used in many fish chowder recipes.

4 fish heads, or bones from 4 fish (any kind saved when fish were cooked for a meal)	2 cups chopped, peeled ripe tomatoes
2 cups water	2 medium potatoes, finely diced
1 small onion, chopped	½ cup minced celery
1 clove garlic, minced	1 bay leaf
2 tablespoons chopped green pepper	1 teaspoon salt
2 tablespoons butter or olive oil	1/8 teaspoon freshly ground black pepper
	1 tablespoon minced parsley

1. Wash the heads or bones and simmer in water ten minutes. Drain, reserving the broth. Pick the meat from the bones and reserve; discard the bones.
2. Saute the onion, garlic and pepper in butter until the onion is transparent. Add the reserved stock, tomatoes, potatoes, celery, bay leaf, salt and pepper to taste. Cook until the potatoes are tender.
3. Add the reserved fish meat and the parsley and reheat.

James Beard's Clam Chowder, 1964

If razor clams, a West Coast variety, are not available for this chowder, do not hesitate to use some other kind. And there will be those who prefer to use about three cups of light cream rather than a quart; either way, the result is a delightful dish with an interesting twist. Serves eight.

Cut 3 to 4 thick rashers lean bacon into rather small pieces and try out in a heavy skillet. Remove the bacon to absorbent paper and pour off all but 2 tablespoons of fat. Saute 1 fairly large onion, coarsely chopped, in fat till it is just transparent. Add 4 smallish potatoes, peeled and diced, and enough clam broth, about 2 cups, to cover. Bring this to a boil. Cook until the potatoes are soft and almost disintegrated. Add salt and pepper to taste and a dash of Tabasco sauce. Heat 1 quart light cream and add potato-onion mixture, bacon bits and lastly 1 ½ cups chopped fresh or canned razor clams. Correct the seasoning. Add ¼ cup cognac, and when clams are just heated through, serve the chowder in hot cups with a dash of chopped parsley. This same chowder may be mixed in an electric blender and served cold with chopped chives and parsley.

A Fish Chowder of Cape Sable, Florida, 1964

"In days past," says Alex Hawkes, *from whose book this recipe comes, a version of this chowder was served at a "peculiar little restaurant" on a "teetering" pier at the village of Flamingo, Cape Sable. This cape is the southernmost point of the mainland in Florida and is now part of the huge Everglades National Park.*

The recipe is fussy, perhaps unnecessarily so, but it leads to a very fine, delicate dish of good proportions. Makes about twelve servings.

4 pounds snapper (or comparable firm fish)	2 cups light cream
2 stalks celery, with leaves, chopped	2 bay leaves
2 large carrots, chopped	2 teaspoons salt
5 sprigs fresh parsley, chopped	½ teaspoon fresh-ground black pepper
2 large onions, chopped	¼ pound salt pork, diced
½ cup butter	1 ½ cups diced onion
½ cup flour	2 cups diced raw potato
2 quarts water	1/8 teaspoon oregano
	6 drops hot pepper sauce

Clean the snapper, cutting the meat into chunks, reserving the bones and head. In a large kettle, place the fish-chunks, bones, and head. Add the celery, carrots, parsley, 2 chopped onions, bay leaves, water, salt, and pepper. Bring to a boil, then lower the heat and simmer until the fish flakes easily when prodded with a fork—usually about 15 minutes. Strain this mixture, retaining the broth

From Alex D. Hawkes, *South Florida Cookery* (Coral Gables, Fla.: Wake-Brook House, 1964), pp. 26–27.

and the fish flakes. Meanwhile, in a skillet saute the diced salt pork until browned. Add the 1 ½ cups of diced onions, and cook until just tender but not browned. Add the fish stock and the raw potato, cooking about 15 minutes, or until the potato is tender. In a small saucepan, melt the butter, gradually blend in the flour, and add the cream. Over low heat, cook this until thickened and very smooth, stirring constantly. Add this roux to the chowder, and next add the fish flakes. Season to taste with salt and pepper, adding the oregano and hot pepper sauce. Simmer for 15 minutes, and serve while very hot.

An Abalone Chowder, 1965

As mentioned earlier, canned abalone can be purchased at Japanese grocery stores. Those who prefer their chowders rather thick should reduce the water and hot milk in this recipe by ¼ cup and ½ cup, respectively. In either case the chowder will be excellent. Serves four to six, depending on the amount of liquid used.

Brown lightly 4 slices of bacon, diced, and pour off all but about 2 tablespoons of the bacon drippings. To the bacon dice add the meat of 6 abalones, which has been pounded and cut into small cubes. Trimmed abalone meat bought at the market is already pounded. Add 1 large raw potato, peeled and diced, 1 medium onion, finely chopped, and 1 small garlic clove, crushed. Saute the mixture until it is golden brown. Add 1 ½ cups hot water, cover the pan, and simmer the mixture until the abalone and potato are tender. Add 3 cups hot milk, 1 tablespoon butter, and salt and pepper to taste. Stir the chowder well and serve it hot.

From *The Gourmet Cookbook*, vol. 2, rev. (New York: Gourmet, 1965), p. 202.

Sour Cream, Potato, and Mushroom Chowder, 1972

In recent times chowders have shown a tendency to become rich, creamy, and possessed of a variety of flavoring agents. This very nice chowder has all three attributes and will especially please all who delight in sour cream.

½ pound mushrooms, coarsely chopped	2 egg yolks, beaten
1 medium onion, chopped	¼ cup sherry
2 tablespoons butter *or* margarine	2 cups dairy sour cream
	Salt, to taste
1 cup raw potato, diced in ½-inch cubes	Pepper, to taste
	¼ teaspoon ground thyme
1 cup boiling water	Dash of ground cloves
2 cups milk	Dash of mace
	Chopped parsley, for garnish

Cook mushrooms and onion in butter in kettle for 3–4 minutes. Add potatoes and water. Bring to boil; cover and cook for 10 minutes, or until potatoes are tender. Add milk; mix next 3 ingredients and stir into first mixture. Heat only to scalding point. Season with salt and pepper; add thyme, cloves and mace. Serve garnished with parsley. Serves 6.

From *Jacksonville Sesquicentennial Cooks' Book*, 2nd ed. (Jacksonville, Fla.: Ambrose the Printer, 1972), p. 34. This recipe is attributed to Mrs. Carle A. Felton, Jr.; the book was compiled by the Sesquicentennial and the American Bicentennial Commission of Jacksonville.

An Oregon Shrimp Chowder, 1972

This is a first-rate chowder of excellent proportions and fine taste. The quantity of onions may seem excessive, but in fact it is not.

¼ cup butter
2 large sweet onions, sliced
1 cup boiling water
4 potatoes, diced
1 ½ teaspoons salt
½ teaspoon freshly ground black pepper

6 cups milk
½ pound grated milk Cheddar cheese (two cups)
2 pounds shrimp, shelled and deveined
3 tablespoons chopped parsley

1. Heat the butter in the saucepan and saute the onions in it until tender. Add the water, potatoes, salt and pepper.
2. Cover and simmer twenty minutes, or until potatoes are tender.
3. Combine the milk and cheese in another saucepan. Heat, stirring, until cheese melts, but do not let boil.
4. Add the shrimp to potato mixture and cook until shrimp are pink, about five minutes. Add cheese mixture and heat, but do not boil. Stir in the parsley.

Yield: Six servings.

From Jean Hewitt, *The New York Times Heritage Cook Book* (New York: G. P. Putnam's Sons, 1972), p. 670. Reprinted by permission.

A Lima Bean Chowder, 1972

This delicious dish is almost a vegetable chowder. Should you use dried lima beans, they should not only be soaked overnight but also cooked for a half hour or more before being added to the other ingredients. The clove of garlic is a desirable part of the dish, but you may never find it—purposely, that is—again. Serves four.

⅓ cup slab bacon, finely chopped	¾ teaspoon salt
1 large onion	¼ teaspoon pepper
3 cups chicken broth	1/8 teaspoon nutmeg
1 cup carrots, cubed	1 large sprig dill weed
2 cups potatoes, cubed	1 clove garlic, peeled and whole
2 cups mushrooms, sliced	1 ½ cups light cream
1 ½ cups lima beans	1 ½ tablespoons butter
Paprika	

Fry the bacon in a large, heavy skillet until light brown. Peel and chop the onion, and saute it in the bacon drippings until it becomes transparent. Add the broth, carrots, potatoes, mushrooms, lima beans, the spices, dill, and garlic. Cover and cook over low heat for 25 minutes. Stir in the cream and simmer for several minutes until the soup is piping hot. Remove the sprig of dill and garlic. Serve the soup hot with a bit of butter and a dash of paprika on each serving.

Bibliographical Note
to the Introduction

The probable origin of the word *chowder* together with some nineteenth-century references to the dish in France appear in *Notes and Queries*, Series 4, Volume 6 (1870), p. 248 and Volume 7 (1871), p. 85. Early uses of the word *chowder* to mean fish-seller, together with the quotation from Tobias Smollett, are in the *Oxford English Dictionary* under "chowder." The reference to an English baked dish of salmon and potatoes as a chowder is mentioned in *Notes and Queries*, Series 4, Volume 4 (1869), p. 307. The chowder feast in New Zealand for the crew of the whaler *Pacific* is described in William B. Whitecar, Jr., *Four Years Aboard the Whaleship* . . . (Philadelphia, 1860), p. 173. Benjamin Lynde's eating of a "chowdered cod" appears in his diary of 1732 as quoted in *American Speech*, Volume 15 (1940), p. 227.

The two works that "borrowed" the chowder recipe from Amelia Simmons's *American Cookery* were: *New American Cookery, or Female Companion* . . . *by an American Lady* (New York, 1805), p. 32, and *The Cook Not Mad, or Rational Cookery* (Watertown, 1831), p. 20. For the chowder discoveries of the

Philadelphian visitor to Boston, see [E. C. Wines], *A Trip to Boston: In a Series of Letters to the Editor of the United States Gazette* (Boston, 1838), p. 79. The boat captain who claimed equality with Daniel Webster as a chowder cook is revealed in Robert Carter, *A Summer Cruise on the Coast of New England* (Boston, 1864), pp. 182–83, and the chowder party given to Prince William Henry is mentioned in *Notes and Queries*, Series 4, Volume 5 (1870), p. 261.

The reference to fishing parties in Boston Harbor is in *The Cook's Own Book . . . by a Boston Housekeeper* (Boston, 1832), p. 51, and the bragging reference to Virginia chowder parties is in Joseph G. Baldwin, *The Flush Times of Alabama and Mississippi* (New York, 1854), p. 80. The huge Rhode Island chowder party of 1848 is mentioned in *A Dictionary of Americanisms on Historical Principles*, edited by Mitford M. Mathews (Chicago, 1960), under ''chowder.'' It was an English traveler, Thomas Colley Grattan, in his *Civilized America* (2 vols.; London, 1859), Volume 1, p. 62, who found chowder ''odious'' but nevertheless held in ''infinite esteem'' in New England. Grattan found a great part of the American scene detestable.

That Nantucket chowders were made without either potatoes or crackers is testified to not only by the chowders from there as given in the text, but also by a Mrs. S. S. Mattocks, who, while not explicitly identifying herself as from Nantucket, offered a recipe for Nantucket Fish Chowder to a Vermont cookbook, adding gratuitously that Nantucket cooks ''never'' put potatoes or crackers into their chowders. Her recipes and comment appear in the *Lyndon Union Club Cook Book* (Lyndonville, Vt., 1909), p. 112. In time, of course, Nantucket cooks found it possible to put both ingredients into their chowders.

Harriet Martineau's experience with what she took to be a milk-based chowder (and indeed *could* have been) is described in

Harriet Martineau, *Society in America* (3 vols.; London, 1837), Volume 1, p. 280. Mrs. E. H. Putnam in her *Mrs. Putnam's Receipt Book* (Boston, 1850), p. 16, used half milk and half water, an early example of a heavy use of milk in chowders. For the gradual increase of milk in New England chowders see Mrs. J. Chadwick, *Home Cooking* (Boston, 1852), p. 84, and Mrs. M. H. Cornelius, *The Young Housekeeper's Friend* (Boston, 1866), pp. 155–56. The Rye Beach chowder, made without onions, is given in *The Premium Cook Book*, edited by Marion Harland (New York, 1894), p. 8.

Eliza Leslie's acceptance of lobsters, crabs, or oysters in chowders appears in her *Miss Leslie's New Cookery Book* (Philadelphia, 1857), p. 88, and an early canned salmon chowder is given in C. S. Richardson and M. E. McClary, *A Collection of Tried Recipes Contributed by Various Malone Housekeepers* (Malone, N.Y., 1882), p. 3.

Mrs. Lettie Lamkin's Texas chowder was contributed to the *Twentieth Century Cook Book* (Huntsville, Texas, *ca.* 1900), p. 8, and the Spanish Chowder offered to the cookbook of the Portia Club of North Yakima, Washington is in the *Cook Book of Favorite Recipes* (North Yakima, 1914), p. 6.

Lastly, some early examples of what would in time be named the Manhattan Clam Chowder appear in: Charles Ranhofer, *The Epicurean* (New York, 1908), p. 269, a work originally published in 1894; the Fulton Market Clam Chowder of 1902 in the text; the Vegetable Clam Chowder of 1929 in *Good Housekeeping's Book of Good Meals* (New York, 1929), p. 131; the Coney Island Clam Chowder in the *Modernistic Recipe-Menu Book*, edited by Jessie Marie DeBoth (Chicago, 1929), pp. 242–43; and the New York Clam Chowder in *Pictorial Review Standard Cook Book* (New York, 1932), p. 71. This last work was copyrighted in 1929.

Index

The titles of specific recipes are printed in italics.